The GIFT of the ETERNAL FATHER

Prophetic Encounters of the Father's Mercy and Prayers

The GIFT of the ETERNAL FATHER

Prophetic Encounters of the Father's Mercy and Prayers

Kathleen Beckman, LHS

Foreword by
Fr. Raymond Skonezny, S.T.L., S.S.L.

PUBLISHING COMPANY
P.O. Box 220 • Goleta, CA 93116
(800) 647-9882 • (805) 692-0043 • Fax: (805) 967-5133
www.queenship.org

© 2005 Queenship Publishing - All Rights Reserved.

Library of Congress Number #2005920748

Published by:
    Queenship Publishing
    P.O. Box 220
    Goleta, CA 93116
    (800) 647-9882 • (805) 692-0043 • Fax: (805) 967-5133
    www.queenship.org

Printed in the United States of America

ISBN: 1-57918-273-9

The Gift of the Eternal Father

Priest Comments on This Book

DIOCESE OF ORANGE
March 19, 2005

The Gift of the Eternal Father by Kathleen Beckman contains inspiring messages with deep and profound meanings that will help the readers to personally sink in the divine Mercy.

The book contains thirty-three encounters that are very much similar to a series of colloquies, which are intimate conversations between soul mates, in their exchange of ecstatic mystical experiences.

Each encounter is deeply woven in the Trinitarian doctrine, profoundly Christo-centric, and enlivened in the Holy spirit. The overall theme revolves around the paschal journey beginning with Passion Sunday and ending with the Feast of Pentecost.

The Gift of the Eternal Father will undoubtedly deepen the contemplative dimension in the readers. I am enthusiastically recommending this insightful and inspiring book to those who are aspiring for the eternal gift of God to quench their spiritual thirst.

Most Reverend Bishop Dominic Luong, D.D., M.S.
Auxiliary Bishop of Orange, California

Priest Comments on This Book Continued

I urge every reader of this book to give prayerful thought to two statements from the documents of Vatican II, regarding the duties and privileges of the laity in their loving concern for their priest-shepherds:

> "By reason of the knowledge, competence of pre-eminence which they have, the laity are empowered—indeed sometimes obliged—to manifest their opinion on the things that pertain to the good of the Church.... This should be done with truth, courage and prudence, and with reverence and charity towards priests, who, by reason of their office, represent the person of Christ" (*Lumen Gentium*, art. 37).

> "The faithful... should share the priests' anxieties and help them as far as possible by prayer and active work, so that they may be better able to overcome difficulties and carry out their duties with greater success" (*Presbyterorum Ordinis*, art. 9).

In these turbulent and disheartening times in the life of the Church, these norms are particularly meaningful. They take on a deeper import, and carry an added mark of authenticity, when those very promptings are reaffirmed by a directly articulated loving manifestation from the heart of God himself, the Father of creation. Through the centuries most of such heaven-spawned revelations are given to his precious flock and their assigned soul-shepherds through God-chosen lay persons; and such revelations typically depict the caring and merciful heart of the Good Shepherd himself. This book represents another collection of such divine love-whisperings. Readers who are open to hearing these whispers with their hearts, will spontaneously respond with their own love-whispers in the ear of the God of love.

Fr. John H. Hampsch, CMF
Claretian Tape Ministry, Los Angeles, California

In these revelations of the Eternal Father given unto Kathleen Beckman is found a beautiful fulfillment of the prayer of St. Paul for the church at Ephesus: "that the God of our Lord Jesus Christ, the Father of glory, may give you a spirit of wisdom and *of revelation in the knowledge of Him.* May the eyes of your hearts be enlightened." (Eph.1:17-18)

May your hearts be permeated with a profound gratitude for the revelation in these pages of heavenly testament of the Eternal Father's love for the Son, for all His children. And may His holy ones cry out through the Spirit of adoption, Abba! Father!

Fr. Joseph Droessler
St. Justin Martyr Catholic Church, Anaheim, CA

St. Paul (1 Cor. 3:1) writes that the spiritual person alone can go from "milk to solid food". In this book, the Eternal Father feeds Kathleen Beckman solid food that is meant to feed the broader Church also. It is timely. As a priest of 45 years, I see the urgent, fundamental need that we have to come before the Eternal Father as His children. *If you seek to know more fully your identity as a child of God, read this book!* It is an experience of the Eternal Father that will take you deeper into the Trinitarian Family and kingdom of the Divine Will.

Fr. Raymond Skonezny, STL, SSL
St. John Neumann Catholic Church, Irvine, CA

With the author, we encounter the Eternal Father in this book and experience His intimate Word poured out for each of us. The majestic voice of love and mercy then, resounds in our hearts with certain urgency. The Eternal Father is speaking to us. Are we listening? *The revelation given here is an invitation into the intimacy of the Most Holy Trinity.* As you respond, you are changed.

Fr. Michael Philen, CMF
Claretian Center, Dominguez, CA

Dedication

This book is dedicated to four loving Fathers.

Pope John Paul II
Father of the Church, Mystical Body

Rev. Raymond Skonezny, S.T.L., S.S.L.
My Spiritual Father and Director

Richard R. Lopez, Sr.
My Father

George B. Beckman
My husband and father of Michael and Christopher

Acknowledgments

I gratefully acknowledge the assistance
of the following people.

Most Reverend Bishop Dominic Luong, D.D., M.S.

Fr. Raymond Skonezny, S.T.L., S.S.L.

Fr. Joseph Droessler

Fr. Michael Philen, C.M.F.

Fr. Michael Sears

The United Hearts of Jesus and Mary Prayer Cenacle

Tommy Canning, Scotland, "The Art of Divine Mercy"

Elissa Fruciano

Marilyn Hollingsworth

Mother Nadine, Intercessors of the Lamb

Bob, Claire & David Schaefer, Queenship Publishing

My family, George, Michael & Christopher

Table of Contents

Chapter One
Thirty-three Encounters with the Eternal Father

Page	Date	Title
2	April 4, 2004	The Paternal Perspective of the Passion of Christ
8	April 5, 2004	Bethany: Hospitality, Friendship, Anointing
11	April 6, 2004	Jesus was Deeply Troubled
14	April 7, 2004	Judas: His Appointed Time Draws Near
17	April 8, 2004	Christ Generates a Kingdom of Priests
23	April 9, 2004	Death on the Cross: His Seven Last Words
31	April 10, 2004	Mary's Holy Saturday Vigil
35	April 11, 2004	Easter: The Alleluia of the Church
38	April 15, 2004	You are Witnesses of These Things
40	April 16, 2004	The Stone Rejected by the Builders
43	April 17, 2004	Their Unbelief: Invoke the Holy Spirit: Proclaim the Gospel
46	April 18, 2004	To Show Mercy
50	April 21, 2004	I So Loved the World
52	April 22, 2004	God is Trustworthy
54	April 24, 2004	Do Not Be Afraid
56	May 30, 2004	In the Upper Room: a New Pentecost
61	June 6, 2004	The Trinitarian Family
63	June 13, 2004	Eucharist: Bread That Comes Down From Heaven
66	June 18, 2004	For Priests: the Heart of the Redeemer
69	July 7, 2004	Seek the Lord
72	July 8, 2004	The Kingdom of Heaven is at Hand
74	July 15, 2004	His Yoke is Easy: His Burden Light

Page		
76	Aug. 6, 2004	I Testify to My Beloved Son
79	Sept. 8, 2004	Mary, Spotless Mirror of the Most Holy Trinity
82	Sept. 15, 2004	Mary's Maternal Cry Pierced the Heavens
86	Sept. 22, 2004	Poverty of Spirit, Personal and Ecclesial: The Priesthood of the Lord
91	Sept. 23, 2004	St. Pio: As If It Were His First, Only And Last Mass
95	Sept. 27, 2004	Whoever Receives This Child In My Name Disrespect for Life
99	Sept. 29, 2004	The Archangels
102	Oct. 5, 2004	Choosing the Better Part: Contemplating Jesus
105	Oct. 6, 2004	"Pater Noster", The Our Father
108	Oct. 10, 2004	The Graces of Healing and Gratitude
111	Nov. 2, 2004	The Divine Will

Chapter Two

Prelude to Thirty-three Encounters

116	July, 1994	A Special Prayer to the Eternal Father
117	Nov., 1994	Paternal Wisdom on Unity in the Church
119	Feb., 1995	Paternal Wisdom on Loving Christ & Resisting the Evil One
120	May, 1995	Paternal Wisdom on America
122	Feb., 1996	Paternal Wisdom on Divine Justice, Divine Mercy
125	Oct., 1997	Paternal Wisdom on Surrender
126	June, 1998	Paternal Wisdom on the Eucharist and Priesthood

Closing Prayers

Page
128 St. Peter Julian Eymard, Eucharistic & Marian Prayer
129 St. Ignatius Loyola, Mystical Intuitions of the Trinity during the Eucharistic Celebration
129 St. Catherine of Siena, The Trinity's Co-presence in the Consecrated Elements
130 The Prayer of Jesus to the Eternal Father, John 17: 1-26
131 The Father's Loving Sacrifice, Meditation on the Gift of God

Illustrations

Sketches by Tommy Canning

http://www.art-of-divinemercy.co.uk

"The Art of Divine Mercy"
Used with permission.

Come and See
I Forgive
Via Dolorosa
The Mother of Tenderness
The Hour of Mercy
I Am the Immaculate Conception
The Holy Family

Preface of the Author

I humbly confide this work to Holy Mother Church in obedience to my Priest Spiritual Director. I find these encounters with The Eternal Father a profound mystery and grace that I should not attempt to explain but entrust to the discernment of the Church.

These graced encounters with Abba, Father began suddenly on Palm Passion Sunday 2004. In each encounter, I was aware of the Eternal Father's majestic, incomprehensible personality bending to me, a sinner. Yet, I was not overwhelmed by this reality because I was graced to understand that He cared very much for me. Each encounter seemed intimate and yet impersonal in that He communicated what seems to be a universal message of mercy.

With all due reverence to The Eternal Father before whom I prostrate, it seemed natural that He would communicate Himself as the loving Father that He is. It was as if I was breathing in the life of The Father just as it was meant to be according to His perfect Divine Will. It seemed to me that Abba, Father desired to communicate His paternal charity to His adopted sons and daughters in yet another way. Of course there is nothing new to be revealed, as the Church has already received the full revelation of God in the person of His Son, Jesus.

Yet, in these encounters with The Father, I was reminded that as a parent of children, I repeat and restate what I am trying to teach my children in many different ways so that they may understand something. Briefly, it seemed that these graced encounters were similar to this. Ultimately, no one can explain the sublimity of God's mysterious ways but I think all would agree that God speaks to His adopted children.

My response to such graced encounters is one of profound gratitude and humility. The gift of the Eternal Father is for me the grace to know Him as my Father and know myself as His little child. This is my identity, freedom and joy. I state these matters in the simplest terms because this is how simple it seemed in these encounters with the Eternal Father. I think this is best understood in the light of the scripture that states, "He called a child over, placed the child in their midst and said, *"Amen, I say to you, unless you turn and become like children, you will not enter the kingdom of heaven. Whoever humbles himself like this child is the greatest in the kingdom of heaven."* (Matthew 18: 2-4)

My prayer is that Abba, Father be glorified in all His children and that we, who have received the gift of life, the gift of faith, come into our true identity as beloved children of God Almighty to be fully alive in His Spirit of Love.

November 25, 2004
Feast of Catherine of Alexandria
Thanksgiving Day, USA

Foreword

Fr. Raymond Skonezny, S.T.L., S.S.L., Spiritual Advisor of Author

As a priest of forty-three years, it is with a profound sense of humility that I am writing the foreword to this book, entitled *"The Gift of the Eternal Father"*. As the author's Priest Spiritual Director, I bring to the readers of this book, a sense of wonder and appreciation for its contents. For a learned theologian or biblical scholar to bring these "encounters" to us would be highly valued and acclaimed. But to have an ordinary person in the Church, a wife and mother, business woman, active in many Church ministries, leading a busy life with family concerns, bring to us these "encounters" with the Eternal Father is truly remarkable: an indication of the Divine Will ordaining mystical favors and charismatic gifts to build up the Church

In the midst of a Church in crisis, God's grace is being showered upon us in various ways. One of these graces is this book and its author whom I have been directing since 1992. I have observed the development of mystical graces in her soul over time and through much suffering. I know the author to be an obedient daughter of the Church, submitting her interior life of grace to the scrutiny and discernment of spiritual direction.

The author of this volume has brought to us a series of "encounters" with our heavenly Father. Surely as Jesus turned to His heavenly Father in prayer and was always in communion with the Father it would seem to be very natural for us to turn to the Father in prayer. However, this is not the common prayer of the ordinary Catholic. It's true that in every Mass the community prays the Our Father together. Every prayer is addressed to the Father directly or through the Son to the Father in the Liturgy of the Church.

Yet, in general, the spiritual life of the faithful concentrates upon the Son of God. It is to Jesus we look and frame our prayers. His birth, public ministry, passion, death and resurrection are the focus of the individual's faith and private prayer life of adoration, contrition and thanksgiving. Prayers of petition and gratitude also reach out to Mary, the Mother of Jesus. Only with the growth of the spiritual life and the movement of the Holy Spirit are we aware of or turn in filial humility and love to the Father. The paternal love of the Father seems to be the goal we reach through the guidance of the Holy Spirit, Who focuses our gaze upon the Son's uplifted Face toward His Father and "our Father." It is then that the words of Jesus, that He Himself taught us what to say in prayer, become full of meaning. What may have become a rote prayer becomes one filled with awe, wonder and love.

It is for this reason that the author's series of "encounters" with the Father are of such tremendous power and interest. Each one begins with the invitation of "Come, listen and write." These "encounters" present to us in a striking manner the paternal mercy and love of the Father. Through her surrender to the Father's invitation, she learns that even with grace, she can only receive a small ray of the divine light of Jesus. Why is that? The Father explains: because all she can ever know and receive is within the confines of her humanity, whereas the Father knows and loves Him without limits and, they and the Holy Spirit are one God.

The Father's love for the Son is succinctly stated in, "The Paternal Perspective of the Passion of Christ" on Palm Sunday as, "He is My love, the Word made Flesh, My Only Begotten Son! Our bond is unbreakable, our love unspeakable and incomprehensible to any human understanding."

With profound seriousness the Father speaks of His Son being sent to bring mankind back into the Kingdom of the Divine Will. The only way to enter that kingdom is "to embrace the 'fiat' of Jesus for oneself, to surrender out of His obedience, to love out of His pierced Heart and live conformed to the Cross in the light of the Resurrection."

The perfect model of one who is in the Kingdom of the Divine Will is Mary, His mother. Probably no other time in the history of the Church is such a model needed. Her 'fiat', surrender, obedience to the Divine Will calls out to the dignity of women today. How timely that the Eternal Father emphasize her maternal role and witness. As Jesus teaches us what it is to be human, to be a righteous man, so Mary is brought before us to show women what it is to be a holy woman before the Father.

Briefly, no foreword can present the value of this work. It brings to us in a very measured and sober presentation of intense spirituality, the Father's relationship to us in Jesus, the Church He founded, in the power of the Holy Spirit, the cost of discipleship, Mary's role, the plan of the Father to bring all into the Kingdom of the Divine Will. Those whose hearts are open to the grace flowing from the pierced heart of the Son must live in this Divine Will. Creation, Redemption, Sanctification arise or flow from this fountain. The coming of the Kingdom in Jesus is the beginning of that Divine Will present in Heaven now manifesting itself upon earth, that all may be one as they are one in the Spirits' bond of love.

None of these "encounters" should be read swiftly but rather in a spirit of prayer and reflection. The sentences are such that one should read one sentence at a time and ponder its meaning before going on. These "encounters" with the Father have an unusual depth and ring of a Father who is desirous of once more asking us to come and listen to His words. This Father is a majestic teacher. Of Him, Jesus will say that all He has heard, He brings to us. His Church is meant to bring these truths, this love, this wisdom into the world.

No one today can minimize the crisis that the world faces in its withdrawal into its self important grandeur. Unity/disunity, love/hate, war/peace are choices on a global scale today. Division is rampant. Who or what will unite the human family? It can only be hoped that all who read these "encounters" of a heart opened by the Father are willing to come to Him, listen to Him and work for that unity to carry out the prerogatives of our merciful Father. We are to become perfect as He is perfect as this is the Divine Will of our loving Father.

May Our Father in heaven surround us with His Son in the bond of the Holy Spirit!

May Mary, our Mother, teach us to listen to the Son that we may hear the Eternal Father! Amen.

Chapter One

**Thirty-three Encounters
with the
Eternal Father**

April 4, 2004 to November 2, 2004

The Gift of the Eternal Father

April 4, 2004 Solemnity of Palm Passion Sunday
The Paternal Perspective of the Passion of Christ

A Personal Introduction

The Eternal Father began, Daughter, come, listen and write. Child, for eight years I have purified you in the crucible of suffering, refined you like gold in the furnace and tested your fidelity amidst hell's fiery darts. Like Job, you have blessed My Holy Name and honored My House. Daughter, of your free will you took up the Cross for love of Jesus and grace transfigured your heart to mirror that of My Son. Your fiat is the key to the kingdom of the Divine Will where you live in a state of surrender participating in the life of the Most Holy Trinity. Now begins a journey of paternal mercy, a grace for you and the members of the Mystical Body who are open. Whoever shall take up and read shall know by the unction of the Spirit, that I am the merciful, Eternal Father bending to reach My prodigal children.

The Paternal Perspective of the Passion of Christ

You will contemplate and live the Passion of Christ this holiest of weeks in and through the Divine Will. I will share My paternal perspective asking you to record what comes from Me for the building up of the Church. I am a good Father generating life for the members of the Mystical Body of Christ that you may live more fully your identity as sons and daughters of God.

Today the Church recounts His triumphant entrance into Jerusalem and His Passion so that you perpetually recall the truth of your redemption born of Trinitarian Charity. May you be moved to reciprocate with heartfelt gratitude and a sacrifice of praise though you shall never comprehend the magnitude of so great an act of love!

Contrast the momentary honor given Him amidst the hailing

with palms and the betrayal that began with a kiss from one of His own. See the fickleness of the human heart and contrast the steadfast Sacred Heart who is fixed on the completion of His mission offering perfect obedience to Me, His beloved Father. He addresses Me from His heart, "Behold, I come to do Your will!"

Today your heart shall be enkindled as I unite you more fully to the kingly, priestly heart of the Redeemer and you partake in the cup of suffering, re-living in your mind and heart the agony to which He was subjected for love of all creatures. Know that I sent Him as revelation of Divine Providence which is that most charitable solicitude of a good father for his children.

He is My Love, the Word made Flesh, My only Begotten Son. Our bond is unbreakable, our love unspeakable and incomprehensible to any human understanding. Today you will try to contemplate the mystery of your redemption and even in the fullness of My grace you will plumb only a small ray of the divine light of Christ, Savior of the world. You know Him and love Him within the confines of your humanity. I know Him and love Him without limits for we are One God, Three Persons: Father, Son and Holy Spirit. I willed to send Him; He willed to obey, suffer and die to redeem humanity. The Holy Spirit willed the revelation of Divine Charity, conceived the Messiah and the Word Was Made Flesh. The Anointed One revealed the countenance of My Holy Face to humanity. In Him you see your Eternal Father's greatest attribute which is mercy. In Him, you see My compassion, fidelity and fulfillment of the divine covenant of charity.

You cannot fathom the depth of paternal charity, the height of My Love in the midst of My Son's Passion when I observed with what zeal He obeyed, with what courage He suffered in the totality of His body, mind and spirit. When I desired to manifest the Face of God to humanity, you creatures who were lost because of sin, I sent Him as the Lamb to be sacrificed once and for all, so that by His Blood you would be ransomed, freed from sin and death. His Blood is My everlasting covenant, the fulfillment of the scriptures that foretold His coming. He speaks only of Me and I am glorified in His sacrifice and victory; glorified in His obedient and humble heart.

I was made to observe the Word Incarnate crucified at the hands of men created by the Divine Will. Remind yourself as you contemplate the Man of Sorrows, that neither the spirit of the world nor the spirit of the netherworld had any power to exercise over the Savior King. It is the Divine Will that exercised all power in the act of Redemption just as the Divine Will exercised all power in the act of Creation. Trinitarian Charity condescended to free humanity of sin and death as all Three Persons of the Trinity agreed on the wood of the Cross becoming the bridge between heaven and earth so you may enter again the Garden of the Tree of Life.

Throughout the hours of the Passion, My Son communicated with me in the Spirit and I was present in His mind's eye except for those moments when it was necessary that I withdraw My consoling presence to complete His sacrifice. I willed the Word Incarnate to feel that He was abandoned by the One whom He loves perfectly, the One whom He cannot be separated from and that is why He cried out, "My God, My God!" He did not utter the familiar name, Abba, Father, because He felt Himself completely abandoned. In that time of utmost desolation, the Spirit of Divine Love was no consolation to Him, so He suffered in His humanity the ultimate torture of dying as if alone and utterly forsaken by His Father God. It became necessary for the Man of Sorrows, the Suffering Servant, to actively unite the faculty of His human will, (fully human) to the Divine Will (fully Divine) for He was the God-Man; but He did not rely on His divinity to lessen His sacrifice. This is what is meant in the scriptures when it states that the Son of Man did not regard equality with God something to be grasped though He was in the form of God. (Phil.2:6)

The kingdom of the Divine Will, the fiat of the human family surrendered to Divine Charity, comes only through Christ Crucified and Risen. Calvary's summit is the only way to freedom for the children of the Most High as His pierced heart is the door to the eternal kingdom. The Word Incarnate was sent to suffer in His body, mind and spirit for He was born to die and rise again to establish my kingdom on earth and open the gates of Paradise. Christ suffered His light to be eclipsed, His breath to be silenced, His love to be spurned, and His body to be defiled as He became sin to save sinners restoring the order of divine love because creation had become disordered by sin.

You live in the light of the resurrection and the sword of the spirit has consecrated you in Truth. But all generations from Adam to The Christ lived in the bondage of death, under the scourge of sin. The demonic legions had freedom to entrap civilizations that awaited the covenant promise of a Messiah as they wrestled under the weight of the old law. He came in the distressing disguise of an ordinary man, poor, humble, obedient, even unto death on a Cross. A sign of contradiction, He became a threat to all authority and in every age, even in the new covenant of His Blood, His authority has been the target of evil doers and rebellious people.

When His hour had come, the hour ordained from the beginning of all ages, Trinitarian authority was handed over to human instruments so they could carry out the predestined judgment of the Divine Will to bring forth the plan of salvation. This is what is meant when Jesus said to Pilate, "You have no power over me except that which comes from Above."

Since that moment in the history of salvation, the incomprehensible tortures of the crucifixion and death of the Anointed One become the perpetual and eternal torture of the Adversary and the fallen legions. The momentary appearance of Divine defeat becomes eternal victory for the offspring of the Trinitarian family. The ways of the Almighty One are far above the human intellect, a mystery to man, perfectly ordained, to undo the cunning intelligence of the Evil One.

I impress these matters upon your soul so that you lay claim to your victory in Christ, so that all My children may know the fulfillment of My Covenant of Love through the Word Incarnate. Every drop of His Precious Blood is the price paid to satisfy the ransom of the human family. It is His Blood that forms the scarlet blanket that covers the earth, each person in it, yet it is for the free will of each person to accept the Gift of God. His tender heart is poured out perfectly, thoroughly, to draw you back into divine intimacies that were lost because of sin. Rare is the man, woman or child who walks to the rhythm of His Heart that beats for you. His merciful heart presses against sinful souls, ungrateful souls, to pardon, almost becoming forgetful of who He is, so as to draw you unto Himself, to carry you back to Me!

At that moment when He was about to expire of ineffable charity, He knew that many would refuse the gift of redemption and mock His Sacrifice to their eternal loss. This pressed heavily upon His anguished heart. His will was fixed on the goal for those who would believe and receive the gift of redemption. The perfection of His charity makes for the perfection of His sacrifice. This is why He could say, "Father, the hour has come. Give glory to your son, so that your son may glorify you." (John 17:1)

The kingdom of the Divine Will consists of a community, a people whose fiat is born of the fiat of the Lamb, whose surrender is born of His obedience, whose love is born of His pierced Heart, whose lives are conformed to the Cross while living in the light of the resurrection. Creation, redemption and sanctification are the Trinitarian aims of the Divine Will for the offspring of the Most High.

Daughter, there is more that I will teach you in these high, holy days when the Church is most radiant with grace. Let silence permeate your heart so you know when your Eternal Father beckons you to "come, listen and write". I bless you, beloved daughter of the Most Holy Trinity, as I embellish your soul with virtues of faith, hope and charity. I love you, The Eternal Father.

Thirty-three Encounters with the Eternal Father

April 5, 2004 Monday of Holy Week
Bethany: Hospitality, Friendship, Anointing

Following Mass and Holy Hour, the Eternal Father began, Daughter, come, listen and write. Dear child of the Most High, the Body of My Son, the risen Heart of the Redeemer, now inebriates your soul and you are prepared to learn from your Father.

Before the Passover, He went to Bethany to enjoy the hospitality of His friends, Lazarus (whom he had raised from the dead), Martha and Mary. In the warmth of this house He found comfort in His friends. He moved their hearts with utterances of His Love. Mary, filled with charity for her guest and Master, broke open that alabaster jar of costly perfumed oil and washed the feet of the Lord, filling that house with the fragrance of extravagant charity, preparing His sacred body for Calvary's summit.

This prefigures the burial anointing of the Crucified One that would take place in a few days' time. The consolation of this communion with friends and apostles will soon give way to the cruel discomfort of His mock trial, condemnation and sentencing to death by crucifixion. Except for the contempt of Judas and Peter's misunderstanding, that supper with friends invigorated His Heart for what was to come. The Word Incarnate is compelled to spend Himself for love of His friends, those in that house at Bethany and those in every age before and after whom He will call friends because they love as He loves. Here you find the essence of the Divine Will. The Holy Trinity is a family of infinite, incomprehensible charity whose nature it is to create more family and communicate love eternally.

Thus the mission of the Redeemer is to reconcile the family of humanity to the Thrice Holy One to open again the door to Paradise; that Garden once lost by the disobedience of Adam, now opened by the obedience of the New Adam and Messiah. The kingdom of the Divine Will is that garden where man and God commune in freedom and mutual self-giving charity that is a perpetual and eternal communion.

Daughter, I formed you for loving communion and all of creation is a testimony to the beauty of the Divine Will. When in sin you were born, the Blood of the Lamb washed over your soul, baptizing you into the eternal covenant of Love. I sent your Redeemer King as a light unto the nations to open the eyes of the blind, to bring prisoners from confinement. He brought forth justice to the nations purchased by His Blood. The Old Law with its heavy yoke becomes the New Covenant of His Blood to set free the family of man, sorely afflicted slaves of sin.

Now behold the Son of Man, Son of God hanging on a tree, crucified like a common criminal pinned there by Ineffable Divine Charity. What return do the nations make to the Lord for His Goodness?

I set before the nations the choice of life or death, truth or the lie, light or darkness. Many nations in this, your time, still choose death, the lie, the darkness. Man has been seduced by the world from the service and worship of God. Your generation suffers much because of sin that breeds hatred and division among the human family. There is a thirst for power and this pride is a deadly sword thrust into the fabric of human existence.

The Church beckons the nations, every person under heaven, unto communion with the Creator. This season of contemplation, repentance and conversion (the Lenten Season) is a recurring universal call to reconciliation. Let the human family turn back to Me through the power and example of the Passion of Christ with its perpetual outpouring of grace from the pierced heart of the Redeemer. My Son remains with you in the humble species of the Eucharistic Host so that you become like Him by the power of the Sanctifier. The soul in the state of grace identifies with the Eucharist and is transformed into bread of life.

The Divine Will is intent upon the reconciliation of the human family. The kingdom of the Divine Will beckons the fiat of humanity toward the sanctification of each person. The fiat of humanity begins with the individual fiat of each person who surrenders in totality to the love of God.

The Crucified One is the Resurrected One who lives and reigns with power as He sits at My right hand in the far more excellent ministry of intercession. Do you know what the Eternal High Priest intercedes toward? He intercedes for the sanctification of the family of man so that His priestly prayer, "Father, that all may be one, as you and I are one", becomes the fulfillment of the act of creation and salvation.

Daughter, during Holy Week, when the Church leads you to contemplate the Anointed One sent to you, when you behold the Man of Sorrows suffering and spilling His Blood for you, reaffirm your fiat to the Divine Will. This will be your prayer and blessing upon the Lamb who was slain for sins. Your fiat is like the breaking open of the alabaster jar of costly perfumed oil, a balm anointing His feet, that part of the Mystical Body that is missionary. Your fiat is a surrender of the heart that is an invitation of hospitality to the Lord. In opening the door of your heart, My Son enters to sup with you and is able to communicate His Love in a heart that is a hospitable abode.

Like Mary of Bethany, do not consider the cost of your fiat for it is the necessary sacrifice for your participation in the passion, death and resurrection of the Lord. Your fiat places you in the center of the Trinitarian family where you are surrounded in creative charity and life of grace. Hospitality is a gift of My Holy Spirit, the fruit of love. I am hospitable, welcoming, always inviting intimacy because of the inexhaustible resources of divine charity.

Let silence reign in your heart being attentive to My call as there is more that I will teach you. Child, this night, I unite your intercessory prayers to the priestly heart of Jesus to draw mercy for the priests gathered around your Bishop at the Solemn Chrism Mass. Your prayers and sufferings are for these chosen sons of the Trinity. I have already said how great is their need for prayer and how deep is My Son's love for these men who perpetuate the apostolic line of His royal priesthood. I bless you with the sign of the Cross. I love you, The Eternal Father.

✝

April 6, 2004   Tuesday of Holy Week
Jesus Was Deeply Troubled

The Eternal Father began, Daughter, having just received Holy Communion, you are full of Eucharistic Love. Now, come, listen and write.

He was deeply troubled as He testified to His disciples, "One of you will betray Me." Now one so close to Him, one whom He loved, betrays the covenant of charity. Self-love breaks the unity of heart and fidelity of friendship inflicting a deep wound unto the Heart of the Redeemer. Here you see how thoroughly Jesus identifies with humanity. The Word Incarnate is completely human and divine: one God, two natures. He took on the fullness of human nature and became like you in every way. He chose to become vulnerable because human nature is vulnerable and therefore His Sacred Heart became completely vulnerable to identify with you.

Man's betrayal began in the Garden of Eden with Adam's sin. Now Judas inflicts the wound in the human heart of the Word Incarnate and Jesus suffers this as a sword that wounds deeply. The Ancient Serpent tempts another person to betray the Lord and moves him like a pawn to do his evil bidding. The free will of Judas is given over to Darkness and the hour of Darkness begins. See the power of a person's free will, the freedom of the person to decide for or against God! Love is a decision of the free will, a surrender of your heart to God first. Your free will is My gratuitous gift and the only gift that you can freely return to Me. Judas's free will became fixed in selfish love that led to His betrayal of the Lord. As guilt overwhelmed him, his free will fixed on despair instead of repentant hope. Since that first Judas, there is a long succession of people who have drawn close enough to the Lord to kiss His holy cheek only to betray Him. The sin of the present generation breeds selfish-love that leads to betrayals, anger, guilt and despair.

The Lamb, My Beloved Son, is soon to be led to the slaughter.

Silence will veil the Lamb because He wills this baptism by fire. He wills it because I will it. He knows the fire that consumes Him will beget the fire of the Spirit and all men will have that freedom to choose eternal life. He wills the gift of the Holy Spirit for humanity at the cost of His Flesh and Blood. He wills to die so you can be baptized into His death and live eternally in the light of His Resurrection. This is the reason for His mission of redemption and yet, in His humanity, He suffers the incomprehensible terror of so horrible a death as crucifixion. The Heart of the Redeemer is tender and not indifferent to human suffering as He takes it upon Himself to pay the debt owed for your sin. His solace is the Divine Will of His Abba. The balm that soothes His Heart is obedience and unity in the Divine Will.

Now Peter says to Him, "Master, I will lay down my life for you." The Lord knows all things and tells Peter the truth. He prophesies, "Before the cock crows, three times you will deny Me." Jesus understands that his friend and apostle now wills to lay down his life for Him but in a few hours he will be weak because the Holy Spirit has not yet descended to empower his free will to stand for Christ amidst the fiery ordeal that will soon surround Jesus and His followers. The Lamb already extends Peter His mercy for He sees the contrition of this apostle and the change that will overcome him in the Upper Room at Pentecost. He knows that Peter is rock of His Church and will indeed lay down his life as the foundation of His Church. Peter would enter into the power of the Holy Spirit on the day of Pentecost when he surrenders his heart in totality to the Divine Will and is surrounded by the Holy Trinity to build upon Christ's foundation, the beginning of the Church. He is chosen to secure for all ages, the treasury of the deposit of faith given through the Person of My Son, to whom Peter gives first witness; a testimony that would eventually lead to his own martyrdom.

The Word Incarnate was sent to earth to proclaim the Good News of salvation for the human family and every word that comes from His mouth is truth for all ages. In every age, the enemies of the truth prevail upon the weakness of the human will. The legions of fallen angels empower persons, families, and nations to disobey the law of divine charity to separate souls from the life of grace, from the service and honor of the Most High. But in your age, there is more cooperation with the fallen angels, more fascination with Darkness because people want to identify with Darkness rather than the Light of Christ. The Deceiver has enslaved many people because their free will has succumbed to his seduction. The Liar tickles the ears of many people and the Truth is pushed aside in favor of what is more pleasing to selfish, sensuous love.

Look closely at the Twelve, the chosen messengers of the Truth, those men of weakness who became strong in the Spirit to carry out the Divine Will of the Trinity. All but one, the youngest, Apostle John, fled the scandal of the Cross. Cowardice overcame them and fear paralyzed their hearts. See the weakness of the human will and the frailty of the human heart. They had yet to yield to the Holy Spirit to become empowered by the gift of Divine Love.

Now the Sacrificial Lamb was about to be offered up once and for all and He was deeply troubled. His Precious Blood would be spilled for the forgiveness of sins. This would make way for the coming of the Spirit to consecrate humanity in Truth so the flames of Divine Love issuing from His Sacred Heart would begin the fire that He longed to start burning on earth. Blessed are you whose sins are forgiven! Blessed is the Innocent Lamb who was slain; whose Precious Blood becomes your covering of grace! In the midst of His darkest hour of agony, He gives His fiat and leads the way for your own surrender.

Daughter, the angel of death, the legions of darkness, are powerless when confronted with a child of Ours whose soul is imprinted with the sign of the Cross; whose free will is surrendered in obedient charity for love of Three In One. I bless you and remind you that silence and peace are the doorways to our communication. In this way I am glorified. Remain in My grace until I call again. I love you, The Eternal Father.

April 7, 2004 — Wednesday of Holy Week
Judas: His Appointed Time Draws Near

The Eternal Father began, Daughter, come, listen and write. His appointed time draws near. Judas Iscariot went to the chief priests and said, "What are you willing to give me if I hand him over to you?" They paid him thirty pieces of silver.

Judas prefigures the many souls in every age who draw near to Jesus and enjoy His friendship for a time and then betray the Lord, forsake Him and enter into the deception of selfish-love. The forces of evil, the Tempter, can knock on the little doors of the human memory and understanding but the Enemy is not permitted to knock on the great door of the human will that is perpetually free to choose right from wrong. Your free will is a protected citadel and you alone give consent to unite to the Divine Will according to your understanding and grace received. You are responsible for each decision and there are many occasions when the spirit of Judas, the spirit of betrayal, is given consent by your free will. Know that charity is the supreme catalyst that drives the human will to choose for the Divine Will. Lack of charity for God causes the free will to choose selfishly and makes impotent the will to love as I love or to value what I value. This is why it is written that you shall love the Lord your God with all your heart, and with all your soul and with your strength. (Deut.6:5) Agape Love is the catalyst that drives your will to choose rightfully.

The Divine Will is the creative and charitable dynamism of the Trinity. You enter only by your fiat; that is your agreement with Divine Charity. See how precious a gift you possess in your freedom to choose Me? It is the nature of agape love to be freely given and freely accepted and therefore your dignity as person is realized, your cooperation is required, not forced.

Judas chose wrongly at every opportunity when choice was given to him and death was his decision. For Judas the Cross was not his difficulty, it was self-love and greed that motivated his free will. Is this not true for your generation? Are not the eternal riches of the kingdom of God exchanged daily for the transitory perishable goods of the world due to pride and desire for power?

The Son of Man will be handed over now. First, He lavishes His Love upon the Apostles at the Passover Meal. The Word Incarnate never missed an opportunity to extend His divine charity and tender friendship upon those who followed Him, especially those chosen men, the Apostles whom He loved completely. He did all He could to prepare them for His Hour, that hour when they would scatter away because they did not understand the mysterious contradiction of suffering required for the Son of Man to ransom humanity. Their imagination took them away because of preconceived ideas of a Messiah King and their concept of an earthly kingdom where they would stand beside Him with authority over many. They willed one thing according to human understanding and the Divine Will of the Trinity possessed the perfect design of salvation. Until the Holy Spirit would illumine their understanding, they could not enter into the wisdom of the kingdom of the Divine Will. Their lack of understanding added to the sufferings of the Anointed One.

Now the Victim Lamb would offer Himself as sacrifice for all. He did not come to be served but to serve and to give His life as ransom for many. (Mt.20:28). His example will pierce the memory and hearts of His followers then and in every age following. The manifestation of the Divine Will in the act of salvation would forever change the course of history and set free the family of man.

The Victory of the Spotless Lamb is manifested in His Resurrection and in the coming of the Holy Spirit. It is given to the Holy Spirit to perpetuate the Lamb's sacrifice, fruitfulness, teaching and victory distributing the unending treasury of graces. Now the doors of your memory and understanding, and the great door of the human free-will can be open to the light of the Resurrected One in the power of the Spirit.

Love consists in this, my child. Not that you have loved Me but that I have loved you first. In the gift of creation, salvation and sanctification, you possess the revelation of Divine Charity that creates, saves and sanctifies. Your fiat to the Divine Will causes you to enter into the creative nature of the Trinitarian Charity, the saving act of the Redeemer and the sanctifying action of the Holy Spirit. Do you comprehend the beauty of the freedom you possess, the dignity of your soul and the effect of your surrender unto Infinite Goodness? As person you enter the Divine Will individually but affect the good of the human family because of the resulting union with the Most High that incorporates all of creation. You become fully human in His humanity to pass into His divinity for this is His prayer that all will be one, as He and I, are one; that you also may be in Us.

It was necessary to send My Only Begotten Son to earth to open that gate to Paradise, to the kingdom of the Divine Will. I fashioned a body for Him, giving a human form to Divine Mercy. His Divine Fiat preceded the human fiat of the Mother of the Redeemer and their combined fiat is your example. Your fiat is that necessary surrender and consent that is the prerequisite to the fountain of grace. If it is grace that you desire, it shall be given unto you for My glory as you surrender. When you choose the better part, you are not denied that which you desire wholeheartedly but enter a communion of living charity.

Daughter, many people have betrayed the Lord for less than thirty pieces of silver. Jesus did not condemn Judas, He loved him to the end but Judas condemned himself by loss of hope which is the ultimate denial of Christ. How many in the present time condemn themselves to a spiritual death for lack of faith, hope and love. The betrayal of Christ continues even among the elect and chosen lot of the priesthood. Those in authority who betray the Lord account for the scattering of the sheep as it is written, strike the Shepherd and the sheep will scatter. Deciding for Christ is costly but deciding for sin is deadly; the sheep and the goats will be separated. The time of decision is now because the hour is late and time presses forward toward the reign of the Holy Spirit in the world, a time of inestimable good for those who stand with Christ.

Pray for the human family. Pray that My Will is done on earth as it is in heaven. Echo the prayer taught by Jesus addressed to Me, His beloved Father. Pray especially for those in authority in the Church, those who have drawn close to Christ for a moment in time, an experience of Love, then turn and betray Him to lead others astray. Many have misappropriated their authority in the name of Christ Jesus causing scandal to Our House.

Daughter, I bless you and bid you to continue to veil your soul in silent contemplation this Holy Week. Be attentive to My call. I love you, The Eternal Father.

✠

April 8, 2004 Holy Thursday
Christ Generates a Kingdom of Priests

The Eternal Father began, Daughter, come, listen and write. On the night He was handed over, He took bread and after He had given thanks, broke it and said, "This is My Body which will be given for you. Do this in remembrance of Me." In the same way also, He took the cup saying, "This is the cup of the new covenant in My blood. Do this in remembrance of Me." This night is like no other and is your saving grace.

The Divine Will manifests now in the institution of the Sacrament of the Lamb's Sacrifice. The Lamb of God consecrates the humble species of bread and wine, instituting the Saving Sacrament, the new and everlasting covenant of His Blood. This covenant perpetuates the Lamb's Sacrifice as living bread come down from heaven for the salvation of the family of man. The Sacrament of His Body and Blood is the flowering of the Divine Will for the human family. You cannot fathom the infinite merits of this August Sacrament nor do you realize with what power it draws you into divine intimacies. With what tenderness My Son extends His priestly heart to regenerate your own!

The Word Incarnate demonstrates His sovereignty at this Passover Supper by stooping to wash the feet of His Apostles. Holy Thursday sets in motion His Perfect Sacrifice. The next day He will wash creation clean by His Precious Blood. But on this unprecedented evening, He stoops in humility to wash the feet of His Apostles to prepare them for priesthood. The one eternal High Priest generates a brotherhood of men to perpetuate His sacrifice and presence on earth to the end of time. These ordinary men, chosen vessels of election, are struck silent and mystified in the presence of the God-man's humble posture before them. He displays vividly what is expected of His brother priests by His merciful example of the fruitfulness of agape love. No one has greater love than this, to lay down one's life for his friends. When they protested the washing of their feet, He said, "Unless I wash you, you will have not inheritance with Me." (John 13:8)

These are the men who become priests in His image, the extension of the Heart of The One Eternal Priest. The Word Incarnate generates a kingdom of priests to serve His House and glorify My Name. He anointed and extended His authority unto them. He entrusted to them the Office of the Priesthood. The High Priest of the new and eternal covenant gives them to share in His sacred ministry and appoints them to perpetuate His Paschal Meal for humanity.

The institution of this ineffable Sacrament of Love is the merciful generation of the Heart of the Redeemer that announces the kingdom of the Divine Will. These sons of Ours; priests, called "alter Christus", have a divine commission to sanctify others and are the backbone of the Mystical Body, the framework of My Temple. Into their hands the Most Holy Trinity places the Body and Blood of the God-man, and whoever eats this Divine Food is regenerated in the image of The Christ to become living sacraments, salt of the earth.

The office of the Priesthood has become diminished in your modern age through the weakness of the shepherds, the influence of the world and assaults of the Enemy. In the mind of God, the Office of the Priesthood cannot be diminished but in the mind of the world, in the mind of the priest, the Office of Priesthood can be reduced to a function and this is not of My doing but of human frailty and sin.

There is a necessary purification that is a cause for hope of a renewed Priesthood for the Church. Whoever is called is given every necessary grace but the sanctity of the entire Mystical Body should be their support. The free will of the priest surrenders unto the Divine Will by yielding to the Holy Spirit in a communion of charity, mirroring The Lamb's sacrifice and victory.

Prayer is that necessary surge of the heart that unites a priest to the One Eternal High Priest. Pray, daughter, for the shepherds of this age who suffer the onslaught of demonic attack and who enter easily into the spirit of the world. Pray that they may become completely identified with their Good Shepherd, Priest and King, realize their dignity before the Most High and become empowered by the Spirit in the service of the Mystical Body. Many priests are in extreme desolation, like dry bones on the desert floor. Pray for the Spirit's breath and living water to revive them and they shall be converted and generate priestly manhood. The lifeblood of the Church flows through them and as the Office of the Priesthood is being renewed by fire, so too the Body of Christ is being purified. The priest who does not identify with Christ Crucified, who boasts in anything except the Cross of Jesus, is living a lie. The priest is first a victim of Divine Love and lives out his victim-hood as another Christ, obedient, pure, humble and holy. Few priests understand their victim-hood for lack of contemplation of the One Perfect Victim, for lack of communion with Him.

He puts in the hands of the priest, the perpetual Sacrifice of the Altar to be the life blood of His Mystical Body. The Church would be born of His Pierced Heart on the summit of Calvary to become the vehicle of saving grace for humanity. My Beloved Son willed the gift of Himself for the redemption of the human family from beginning to end. With every fiber of His being, fully divine and fully human, He lived His fiat that I may be glorified in Him.

Daughter, Divine Love is perfectly ordered to the creation, salvation and sanctification of the human family. The Word Incarnate becomes the Perfect Sacrifice for all time and eternity. The Divine Will of the Trinity creates the environment necessary for eternal communion of man with God. The decision becomes a personal one as your free will is the key to the door of the kingdom of the Divine Will, the kingdom of incomprehensible Trinitarian

Charity.

When you decide for My Son, your reciprocal love draws the grace of wisdom, knowledge and understanding by the power of the Holy Spirit. This guest of your soul moves your memory to recall the good I have done, moves your understanding to know Me, your Father, through the Person of My Son. This creates a spiritual environment for knowing and loving your Creator. Your free will can choose to live in the Divine Will and this decision becomes the means of mutual possession in an incomprehensible union of heaven (Creator) and earth (creature) in your soul. This is how the fulfillment of the prayer of Jesus, "Father, your will be done on earth as in heaven," is being realized. Your will becomes drowned in Divine Charity so you live and move and have your being in Him, My Son. This is the will of your Father in heaven, to see My Son in you, in every person created in love and made new in His Blood, sanctified by the Holy Spirit. Then will heaven and earth move in the rhythm of one heartbeat of Charity.

Daughter, rest this night in the heart of the Blessed Virgin Mary for she is to prepare you to enter into tomorrow's remembrance of the Passion of My Beloved Son. You are surrounded in My paternal affection and blessing. I love you, dear daughter of the Trinity, The Eternal Father.

My Prayer: Interceding For Priests

Abba, Father, be glorified in the men who follow in the apostolic line of your Son's royal priesthood. I pray for all priests on this Holy Thursday when the Church recalls with gratitude the institution of the Sacraments of the Eucharist and Holy Orders. As Jesus humbled Himself to wash the feet of His Apostles, I desire to imitate my Lord and wash their feet with tears of gratitude. When I behold at the Altar of Sacrifice, an ordinary man, stamped with the extraordinary seal of the Priesthood of the Lord, I am moved to tears of joy, mindful that without this priest, I would not receive the seven fold sacramental fountain of grace for the journey back to the Fatherland.

Father, in these times, I observe broken hearted priests, so many disillusioned men who know not their dignity as vessels of election. Could my tears of sorrow become a healing salve to soothe their wounds? The spirit of the world laid traps and many were ensnared. Yet, in the countenance of their faces, I see still a desire to seek after Christ, to put their arms around the Cross, and live His charity at the cost of laying down their lives for the Gospel.

Father, I pray for all priests to receive the grace of transforming union in Christ Crucified and Resurrected: that they may know, love and serve you, Abba. By your grace, cause them to mirror the Redeemer's Heart for the Church. Please make of me, a sacrificial, intercessory vessel of mercy for the Priesthood. Permit that I draw living water, the Holy Spirit, to quench their thirst and strengthen their ministry. May my life be an intercessory prayer for them?

You entrusted me unto Mary's Immaculate Heart this night so that she can prepare me to enter contemplation of the Lord's Passion on Good Friday. I pray that I may be another little handmaid interceding on behalf of all priests. She has already taught me to pray for them: that they will pray, experience the love of the Spirit and receive their personal Pentecost. She has asked me to carry them mystically into the Upper Room to receive the fresh anointing of the Holy Spirit.

Father, I pray that they are carried by grace to the summit of prayer to become like John, the Beloved, who rested his head upon the heart of Jesus on that first Holy Thursday. In your mercy, capture their hearts again. Grant graces of wisdom, knowledge and understanding so they reclaim lost territory for you. May their hearts be the targets of your paternal affection and grace! May I tread the winepress to bring forth new wine in the priesthood? Breathe your Spirit into the brotherhood of priests and bring them to new life in your divine charity. May I be a vessel of mercy for them? This is my prayer. Amen.

The Gift of the Eternal Father

✞

April 9, 2004 Good Friday
Death on the Cross; His Last Seven Words

The Eternal Father began, Daughter, come, listen, write. Today the Universal Church immerses herself in the remembrance of the incomprehensible Act of Salvation, the Passion and Death of My Beloved Son, Savior of the world. Today, the prophecy of Isaiah already fulfilled, is prayed in every Liturgy of The Word. "See, My servant shall prosper, he shall be raised high and greatly exalted. Even as many were amazed at him, so marred was his look beyond human semblance and his appearance beyond that of the sons of man, so shall he startle many nations, because of him kings shall stand speechless; for those who have not been told shall see, and those who have not heard shall ponder it." (Is. 52:13-14)

Daughter, confide today's Liturgy of the Word into your memory, permitting My Spirit to engrave it upon your heart so that it remains like a gem adorning your heart. "Though He was harshly treated, he submitted and opened not his mouth; like a lamb led to the slaughter or a sheep before the shearers; he was silent and opened not his mouth." This prophecy foretells the fiat of the God-man amidst His cruelest sufferings. The silence of the Lamb is a revelation of the perfection of His fiat to the Divine Will, a "yes" shrouded in silence that can never be silenced. He surrendered Himself unto death in silence that speaks throughout salvation history. The Lamb is fixed on obedience in unity with the Divine Will as His entire Being agonizes throughout His tortuous death by crucifixion. He is filled with Charity's most ardent desire to complete the mission entrusted to Him: to free prisoners of sin and open the gate to the eternal Garden of Eden. By the power of His fiat to die on the Cross, to be raised up on the Wood, He draws all things unto Himself and the kingdom of the Divine Will bridges heaven and earth. The Cross is more than suffering and humiliation because of its salutary effects. It is the anticipation of the glory of My Son. Thus, He moved toward the Cross with zealous and majestic assuredness.

His First Word

"Father, forgive them for they know not what they do," becomes His foremost testimony to Divine Mercy teaching humanity the model of forgiveness. He had already taught His apostles the prayer, "Forgive us our trespasses as we forgive those who trespass against us." From the Cross, the Savior intercedes for humanity and His prayer pierces the minds and hearts of His persecutors at that moment and extends to the end of time.

Forgiveness is born of your desire to love as He loves, so you can will to forgive as He forgives. Many can not enter the Kingdom of the Divine Will because they harbor un-forgiveness rendering them unable to love or to receive mercy from their Merciful Father because they do not extend mercy to others. Commit to your memory His first words from the Cross as they were expressed in excruciating pain at the peak of His appointed hour and ardently desired by the Redeemer to be an example for you to imitate.

The utterance of My Beloved Son moved Me to render mercy upon all who have crucified Him. He mediated that grace for you as a perpetual indication of Divine Mercy for souls. He had completely identified with your humanity and desired that you identify with His Divinity becoming a dispenser of Divine Mercy.

His Second Word

"Today you will be with Me in Paradise", becomes his second testimony to Divine Mercy on Calvary, revealing the magnanimity of the Divine Will. In return for a repentant criminal's act of faith, Paradise is awarded the Good Thief on the Day of Redemption. The Good Thief prefigures the conversion of repentant sinners throughout history. The kingdom of the Divine Will is a fount of mercy. There are two gushing fountains of mercy springing forth on Calvary's Hill for His disciples: the Blood of the Lamb and the Water of the Spirit. From the Cross comes new life; the pierced Heart of the Redeemer as an endless wellspring of love for those who come to receive grace from His Priestly Heart.

He is the perpetual libation that gives life to humanity, watering the earth with hope. His response to the Good Thief as He hung on the Cross reveals the tenderness of His Heart so readily moved to grant mercy. He desires to lavish mercy upon sinners as He wills to be in loving communion with each man, woman and child. So beloved are you to Him, that He gathers you unto Himself to carry you to Me. That is why He said, "Father, I do not wish to lose one of those You have given unto Me." His tender mercies toward you move My heart to appease divine justice.

His Third Word

"Woman, behold, your son. Son, behold your Mother", bestows a most unique and efficacious gift to humanity. The masterpiece of the Divine Will is Miriam, Mother of the Word Incarnate, Mother of the Lamb, Mother of the Church, Mother of the cosmos, and Mother of each son and daughter of the Trinity. The one, perfected human creature, incomparable to any other human being, is given now, to each person as gift in the highest order of grace.

In the mind of the Trinity she was perfected and born into the world at the appointed time, preserved entirely for the designs of the Divine Will. The whole of creation awaited her fiat (yes, she was entirely free) to set into motion the Incarnation of the Word and the Salvation of humanity. I tell you solemnly, her words at the Annunciation, "Let it be done unto me according to your word", are highest wisdom and key to living the Divine Will. She lived these words throughout her lifetime and perpetuates them throughout history. This masterpiece of Trinitarian Charity is the Queen Mother of all creation who has never lived one moment outside of the kingdom of the Divine Will. She, who remained with the Lamb mystically, in every torture of the crucifixion, desired only God's Will, because she is always surrendered unto the Most Holy Trinity. She is the Mediatrix of all grace; the purest vessel of blessing for humanity. No heavenly grace descends upon earth except through her maternal mediation by the design of The Most Holy Trinity.

Devotion to the Mother of the Redeemer gives honor to Me, as no other creature glorifies My work of grace like Miriam, the Immaculate Conception. At the foot of the Cross, when she desired to lavish her love upon her only Son and Savior, she was instructed to extend maternal charity to all the sons and daughters of the Lord and she loves you, as she loves her son, Jesus. She loves without distinction because this is what Jesus asks of her. She, above all, emulates her Son and is obedient to do whatever He tells her. No one comes to Me except through the Son but she is the vehicle that carries you most directly to the Son so He can bring you to Me. On earth you will never comprehend the unity of the Mother and the Son. Seek to enter into the inseparable Two Hearts. There exists the sweetest love.

His Fourth Word

"My God, my God, why have you forsaken Me?" indicates His complete identification with humanity and His total surrender to paternal providence. On the Cross, the interior agony of spiritual abandonment was afforded My Son as part of His unity with human suffering. He was made to cry out so you will know how thoroughly the Son of God identified with human frailty, so that no one despairs in the darkest hours, but unites to His agony, to be carried through death into His resurrection. His sorrow was to console all sorrowful men, women and children unto the end of time. That moment of His desperation was complete so that you might have hope. The Divine Will is never a matter of despair but always a matter of hope and this comes from faith in Him. He cried out for Me when His Breath was almost spent. It was from the depths of His Sorrowful Heart that He reached for His Father because of the love that exists between Us in the communion of Our divinity. His fourth word portrays servitude and humility that permeated His Being to the glory of My Holy Name. This is why He was sent to earth: to glorify His Father and your Father, by doing My holy will. He reconciled you to Me, making you heirs to the kingdom, a kingdom I conferred upon Him because He glorified Me in all things. Especially in the agonizing moment when He was about to expire for love of you, He was made to feel that He had been forsaken even by His Beloved Abba.

His Fifth Word

"I thirst", not only represents the intense physical dehydration He suffered during the crucifixion, but the incomprehensible mystical thirst of the Heart of the Redeemer. As much as His Body needed water, His Heart was dying of thirst for souls. He desired to bring the lost children of the world into the Paradise prepared for you, opened again by His Perfect Sacrifice. The Blood flowing from His pierced Heart is to satisfy your thirst for Him. He anticipates and supplies for all your spiritual welfare because He is all Love.

He knew that He had satisfied the debt of humanity and would no longer remain on earth in the midst of those He loved. He knew that it was the appointed time to return to His heavenly kingdom so the Holy Spirit could descend into the newborn Church. His Mystical Body was about to be born and the Spirit was ready to perpetuate the sanctification of redeemed humanity. He ardently desired to start the fire of the Spirit on earth! He willed to manifest His unquenchable thirst so that you would thirst also and come to drink deeply of His ineffable love. You alone can satisfy His thirst and He alone can satisfy your heart. This is the reality of the communion He purchased for you, in the greatest charitable act of laying down His life for His friends. In this, your age, His thirst persists because His love is spurned still. I ask, "Is your thirst satisfied yet?"

His Sixth Word

"When the Savior speaks from the Cross, "It is finished", His exalted task completed, He proves Satan wrong about condemnation and death. These were the words that confirmed for Satan that Jesus of Nazareth, Son of Mary and Joseph, is the Son of God. As an angel of light, Lucifer had knowledge of the Divine Plan to save humanity. But the hidden, humble Word Incarnate was veiled in the disguise of a poor man, without stately bearing, one who was spurned and held in no esteem. When the Adversary heard Jesus speak the sixth word from the Cross, the Enemy of the offspring of

God understood: he was defeated by the Blood of the Lamb. This is the Blood that he so vehemently willed to be spilled, inciting the enemies of Christ to utmost cruelty. Now he realizes that his crafty intelligence has been confounded!

The words, "It is finished." is a victory statement indicating the completion of His Sacrifice, the priceless payment for the ransom of humanity. He speaks of the fulfillment of the plan of salvation, and defeat of the Enemy. The mission of the Redeemer is complete and the dawn of a new day begins. By the saving power of His Blood, the glory of Easter is soon to appear. All this for love of His Father! All this for love of creatures! Even those who would remain outside the Gift of God and lay no claim to the inheritance won for you.

It can be understood that you each have a mission within the Mission of the Redeemer and at the end of your life, when you pass from what is physical to what is pure spirit, you will know the finality of His words. "It is finished" will then be understood by you. Now, you must run the race to the finish line and only those who persevere to the end, receive the crown of everlasting life. Many begin the mission of co-redemption and fall short of the finish line. But Love endures all things and never fails.

His Seventh Word

"The salvation of mankind is consummated. He utters His seventh word from the Cross, "Father, into your hands, I commend My Spirit." He directs His prayer to Me because we are perfectly united in one understanding, will and love. In the perfection of our unity I receive His Sacrifice as part of the divine fruitfulness.

He gives up His breath but His Saving Act shall breathe life into humanity unto the end of time. The Lamb of God is slain and enters into the valley of death to overshadow it with new and eternal life. The reconciliation of the family of man into the embrace of the Trinity is made complete by the spilling of His Precious Blood. The Word Incarnate is returning to My Right Hand, glorifying Me as I glorify Him. He has made My Name known and revealed My merciful countenance. I pronounce all things to be under His divine judgment: sovereignty is His! The Lamb slain is the victorious Lamb and the King of glory. I, The Eternal Father, confer My kingdom unto Him. My Son restores creation to the most charitable order of the Divine Will by His passion, death and resurrection. The greatest of solemnities in the Church, the Resurrection of the Lord, is the seal of the victory of the Cross. Apparent defeat gives way to eternal victory.

Daughter, you will soon celebrate Easter but now contemplate the price of your salvation; the Blood that washed you clean. Thank your Redeemer with songs of gratitude arising from your heart. Allow yourself to be captured by the mystery of your Redemption and spiritual adoption into the family of the Most Holy Trinity. Keep in your heart every word uttered from Him as seeds of contemplation. Then strive to live His words and imitate His gift of self. Keep "Good Friday" before your mind's eye and it will be a source of perpetual wisdom and life for your soul. Accepting His Perfect Sacrifice as a personal gift, your heart will enlarge in reciprocal love for Him. Remember that He is your Savior who becomes vulnerable on the Cross so that you become vulnerable in return because intimacy with His Heart requires the complete entrustment of yourself unto the divine will, Father, Son and Holy Spirit.

Your Holy Mother is present to you now. Honor her also. Her passion was mystically suffered but her pain was complete. It would have been easier had she been permitted to expire with Her Son. She strengthens and prepares you for more. She journeys with the Church toward resurrection, magnifying the prayers and sacrifices of the faithful in the refulgence of her splendor.

I love you, The Eternal Father.

The Gift of the Eternal Father

✞

April 10, 2004   Holy Saturday
Mary's Holy Saturday Vigil

In the evening at my home, the Eternal Father began, Daughter, come, listen, and write. The Body of Christ lay in the tomb and the world was shadowed except for the light of the Immaculate Conception, Mary, mother of the Lamb who was slain. Saturday was the festival day of rest as prescribed by the law. Mary, who kept all things in her heart, contemplated the sacrifice of her Son, relieved that He suffered no more this day. She prayed in expectant faith of His Resurrection. Wisdom illumined her mind and heart to know that He had ransomed the sin-sick children of God and that salvation history would climax on that first Easter morning!

She awaited their reunion, anticipating with what ineffable Love He would greet His mother and how her joy would be complete in His presence again. Flesh of her flesh and bone of her bones, a resurrected Redeemer whose body was glorified now, would soon come to her. In this reunion of mother and Son, He would heal the wounds inflicted from the thrust of the seven swords that pierced her maternal heart. Their Two Hearts would join together in the joy of the Divine Will, His victory over death and evil in the perfect plan of salvation.

Daughter, your Holy Mother was never anxious or fearful. Perfected in grace by the design of the Divine Will, her charity is perfect and fear cannot exist in the environment of perfect charity. Her fiat is perfectly conformed to the Divine Will as she surrendered her will to Mine, making herself a complete gift to the Most Holy Trinity.

But suffer, she did! She willed to suffer as He suffered and she is called the Queen of Martyrs because she was martyred with Christ, mystically experiencing the Passion in every aspect of His suffering. Hers is a white martyrdom but it was more painful than had she been permitted to die physically with her Son on Calvary's

Hill. Simeon's prophecy was fulfilled and seven times a sword pierced her Immaculate Heart. That final sword tore at her heart as she held that lifeless Sacred Body in her arms and then buried the fruit of her womb. She willed His complete self immolation yet she suffered incomprehensible agony of the spirit that brought her to the brink of expiring also.

    Her obedience of faith, her infused wisdom set the standard for that shaken early Church. On this day, the apostles and holy women would find their mother praying and she would strengthen their hearts and console them. She is a great comfort for all who draw near to her, then and now. She was full of peace and tried to impart this peace unto the shaken apostles and friends of Christ. Now, it is under her mantle that the newly born Church is gathered and protected. Her maternal counsel was like milk for the early Church. They were drawn to her radiance, that light of faith that shone from her being for all to behold as a sign of solidarity with her Son. Her heart, so full of charity, drew them like a magnet. They marveled at her wisdom and courage, beholding a mystery in her. She served them all, the apostles who made their way back to her and the holy women who wept and could scarcely be consoled. Their faith was small and their hopes dashed away on that hill of Calvary but they loved Him still. How much they needed their Holy Mother this day!

    Dawn would bring the good news of the Resurrection and He would reveal Himself, His glorified Body, to His friends. Daughter, words fail to describe that first reunion of My Son with His mother for such an exchange of Love cannot be expressed in human terms, the language of such perfect affection is too lofty for human ears.

    The Masterpiece of the Trinity is the Mother of the Word Incarnate and she is the chosen instrument of the Divine Will, the Cooperator that makes fruitful the Will of the Trinity in the plan of creation, salvation and sanctification. She is the Queen Mother of the Kingdom of the Divine Will and until the end of time her maternal mediation affects the family of mankind. She is the Coredemptrix who willed to participate in the complete sufferings of Her Redeemer Son and who remained with Him as He became the

Lamb who was slain. Hers was an unspeakable interior agony united to the Savior's sacrifice for she chose as He chose: the immolation of His Body, the drinking of the chalice in totality.

The Immaculate Conception is given to humanity as Mother, holy, humble, obedient, and pure, reaching out to you, to the Church, in unceasing intercession for the needs of all men, women and children. Every nation is under her maternal mantle of love and only in heaven will you know fully the extent of her maternal mediation. She, who is the spouse of the Holy Spirit, now works toward the sanctification of all who have been purchased by the Blood of the Lamb. She, above all other creatures, realizes the price He paid for you and knows well the cost of your Redemption. She is ever mindful of His Sacrifice, having participated mystically with Him. Now she assists you to be mindful also. She models for you, the art of reciprocal charity for Him.

Her fiat to her Creator made possible the Incarnation at the time of the visitation of the Angel Gabriel. Her soul at Calvary magnified the Sacrifice of the Lamb. Her unfathomable union with the Holy Spirit marks the sanctifying action of the Spirit with the maternal beauty of Holy Motherhood. The family of man will find in her the consolation of Maternal Charity, the wisdom and strength of a mother warrior. She is now the Mother of the victorious Lamb. She is the woman clothed with the sun, crowned with twelve stars, whose heel bears down upon the head of the ancient serpent. Yes, the Enemy fears her presence!

On this day of rest and prayerful anticipation of the New Dawn, she offered her hymn of praise as she did that day at Ein Kareem with her cousin, Elizabeth. It is finished, His mission accomplished and she raises her weary heart with its seven wounds and offers praise to the Most Holy Trinity. She knows He lives!

Daughter, thank you for being attentive to My call to come, listen and write. Rest now in the arms of your holy Mother and give thanks. I love you, The Eternal Father.

The Gift of the Eternal Father

✝

April 11, 2004 Easter Sunday
Easter: The Alleluia of the Church

 The Eternal Father began, Daughter, come, listen, write. The alleluia of the Church born of His Pierced Heart resounds to the heavens on this greatest of feast days celebrating the Resurrection of the Lord. There is cause for rejoicing among the children of God on this day recalling His perpetual victory over death and sin. The Church Triumphant receives your hymns of praise and prayers of gratitude as a column of incense rising from earth to the heavens. The Spirit leads the Church from glory to glory and today's Feast is a glorious day of divine grace showering creation. The Resurrection is the glorification of My Son and My divine seal on the act of salvation accomplished on the Cross. Now the stone rejected by the builders becomes the cornerstone!
 The liturgical celebrations of the Universal Church on this Easter Sunday fill the Body of Christ with hope of new life in Him. He has created a holy people for Himself and gathers you in the wake of His Resurrection. After forty days of contemplating the Suffering Servant, the Passion of the Lamb, after three High Holy Days of traditional ritual and prayer, (The Triduum), the Church honors the Risen Lord, His glorious Body bearing testimony to the great miracle of Resurrection, the climax of salvation history.
 Today the Church is filled with renewed hope for He Who Is Risen is truly Jesus of Nazareth! The grace of the liturgical seasons carries the soul of the Church back to the foundations of Truth and rekindles the fire of Divine Charity in the hearts of her members by living the liturgical cycles that point to the old and new testaments of the Word. Christ is the resurrection and the life so that whoever believes in Him, even if he dies, shall live. This is the mystery of your life in and with Christ.
 Today many people approached the Altar of Sacrifice to receive the August Sacrament of the Risen Lord with newfound desire for deeper union with My Son, for the Spirit has rekindled

many hearts in this holy season of Lent. Within the human heart is a longing for the kingdom of the Divine Will; union with the Beloved that is Paradise.

The Church, in the power of the Holy Spirit, has made Him known to the four corners of the earth proclaiming the Gospel to those who have ears, transfiguring disciples into His image. To all the nations the Spirit proclaims the act of salvation with the offer of the olive branch echoing the words of the Redeemer, "My peace be with you." The glories of My Son, His mission of salvation, resound unto the ends of the earth but many are blind and deaf and attribute to themselves what comes from Him. But He is intent on the unification with Divine Will and His pierced heart bathes souls to spiritualize them so many will imitate His complete surrender to the will of His Father.

Daughter, pray for the Church especially those who returned after long absences and the newly professed who came to the waters of Baptism. What drew them? The Sufferings of the Lamb, the Passion of My Son, continues to break open hearts and shatters barriers. The Resurrection is cause for hope, a perpetual light in the darkness of the world as signified in the Easter candle that burns in the sanctuary near the Altar of Sacrifice as a continuous reminder of today's promise. The dangers of your present age give rise to fear but the promise of the resurrection dispels all fear because it is the manifestation of His life on earth that culminates in the perfect act of divine charity. You come to realize that He who said to His Apostles, "Be not afraid", remains with you in steadfast love that casts out fear.

After recognizing His voice, Mary of Magdala ran to Simon Peter and the Beloved John, that first Easter Morning. John arrived at the tomb before Peter but Simon Peter was the first to see the empty tomb and burial cloths. John believed though he did not understand. They bore witness of the empty tomb to the other apostles and friends of Christ. In their minds they recounted the profound events of the past few days attempting to comprehend something of what they had witnessed. They helped one another to recall and retell what they had seen and heard.

Jesus began to appear to His chosen witnesses up to the time of His Ascension into heaven. He allowed them to see and touch, manifesting Himself in familiar ways like the sharing of a meal, so they came to recognize Him though He was now in the state of glory. The Risen Lord appeared to His apostles to reinforce the Church's foundation, to solidify faith in His Resurrection, giving evidence of His mastery over life and death; demonstrating His sovereignty and they came to believe and spread His gospel.

The perpetual grace of His passion, death and resurrection is the Church's sevenfold sacramental fountain of grace that renews the earth in His Life. Those who drink deeply of the Sacramental life in the Church become like Him and your witness is credible because of your union with Him. You become a living gospel and your authenticity is sealed in the sign of the Cross. The sanctifying action of the Holy Spirit brings forth a renewed humanity and is already moving you in the light of the Resurrection, toward the springtime of fidelity to My Holy Will.

I, too, desire the fulfillment of the prayer He taught, "Father, Thy will be done on earth as in heaven." Your free will is the highest human faculty and distinguishes you from all other creatures. When you surrender unto the Divine Will, you enter the full promise of the resurrection and live in Him as He carries you back to Me because His aim is always reconciliation. Incomprehensible is the mutual outpouring of divine charity between Us and His satisfaction rests in Me as My divine fruitfulness rests in Him.

I sent Him and He came that you might have life in abundance. But the most efficacious fruitfulness of the Spirit has not yet been received by all. It is from the kingdom within that you become the salt of the earth, leaven for the Church, and His mirror image. As I see Myself in the Word Incarnate, I want to see you in Him. This is what it means to have abundant life: the incorporation of your life in His. The grace of the Resurrection is to expand your heart, mind and will, into the unfathomable expanse of His Heart, to be carried by Him into My gates!

Daughter, this day you lived the grace of the Resurrection with your family and received blessing from My Almighty Hand. In your service to them, I am glorified. You extend my merciful love for your family and I address the spiritual poverty of your household. I love you, dear daughter of the Trinity. Keep gazing upon My Son so you become like Him and I shall be pleased. The Eternal Father.

✟

April 15, 2004 Thursday of the Octave of Easter
You Are Witnesses of These Things

The Eternal Father began, Daughter, come, listen and write. Jesus said to them, "These are My words that I spoke to you while I was still with you, that everything written about Me in the law of Moses, in the prophets and psalms must be fulfilled." Then He said to them, "Thus it is written that the Christ would suffer and rise from the dead on the third day and that repentance, for the forgiveness of sins, would be preached in His name to all the nations, beginning from Jerusalem. You are witnesses of these things." (The Gospel of the day: Luke 24: 44-48)

Daughter, My Son commissions witnesses of His passion, death and resurrection to preach repentance for the forgiveness of sins to all the nations. He prepares and commissions a continuous line of witnesses to perpetuate His stupendous act of charity in the redemption of mankind. This is how faith in Him would spread and the Church's foundation would be secured. His disciples grew in number through the preaching of the apostles and the testimony of witnesses of these things.

Today also the Church continues to grow through the preaching of the Gospel by the continuous apostolic line of His Priesthood. The life of the believer is not isolated but unfolds in the presence of a multitude of witnesses that encourage you to fervor. These are not only the living but those who have preceded you in faith. Great witnesses are the believers who know My Son's life, death, and resurrection by their experience of His inexhaustible charity. Whoever believes in Him bears witness to Him. Love Him as He first loved you so your witness springs forth from your communion with Him.

The art of loving is perfected in the unity of the Most Holy Trinity and My Son bears witness to My paternal charity so you come to know your most merciful Father in heaven. To bear witness to Christ is your duty as one who believes in Him. The gift of God that you have received must be given to others because faith, hope and love are not fruitful until they are expressed to others. To be a witness of Christ is the fruit of agape love, always giving life to more love.

His Mystical Body is perpetually dying and rising in Him, making fruitful His saving act of salvation. Participation in His resurrection comes through sacramental baptism into His death as the seal of salvation. In His sufferings He sanctifies the suffering of the Mystical Body and establishes a covenant of everlasting life for those who believe and hope in Him. His Sacrifice made you adopted sons and daughters and carried you, Our prodigal children, back into the bosom of your Father. I embrace whomever He brings to Me and make known My love for you.

The persecution of the Church is a sign of her authenticity. According to the spirit of the world and enemies of the Church, you are foolish to believe in the Gospel, foolish to witness to Him. But the humble ones are chosen to confound the proud.

A great struggle persists between Christ and the anti-Christ, the Church and the anti-Church. The Church makes her journey toward glory but continues to suffer persecution along the steep and narrow road that leads to eternal reward. As legions attack the Mystical Body from within and without, you remain as His witnesses. The smoke in the Sanctuary suffocates the faith of many. The apostasy continues even among those in authority who forsake Jesus to live a Gospel stripped of the Cross, a compromise of the Truth. Many are led out of the Church by those who bear false witness to My Son. Compromise of the Gospel cheats humanity. The revelation of Truth is ordered in the Divine Will and perfect in its entirety. Presented in part, it is not whole and the fullness of Divine Charity is denied. The Holy Spirit is the necessary agent of the Truth and Counselor of the wise.

The Gift of the Eternal Father

As the spirit of the world and enemies of the Church press against Her, the Holy Spirit anoints a spiritual family to combat the forces of darkness and defend the honor of My Name. The Divine Will is realized through the obedient witnesses of the Truth. You do not suffer in vain while working toward the dawn of the new day. The everlasting covenant of His Blood is the promise of resurrection and life, on earth and in heaven.

Mary, Mother of the Church, oversees your purification and makes fruitful the work of the Spirit toward restoring the Church to a house of prayer, cleansing the sanctuary of the Evil One who strives to tear down what was built by My Son. A little while longer and the angelic trumpets will sound to arouse more witnesses to rise up as mystical soldiers of Christ, to defend the evil onslaught against Our House. Extrinsic evil will be pushed back. The intrinsic evil of sin will always require your need for Grace and heaven will provide what you need.

Under Mary's mantle of holiness, the Church is protected, growing and moving toward triumph. Through her maternal mediation the splendor of Truth shall manifest spiritually but tangibly. Many then will come to believe in Him and enter the Church to be blessed. For all people, the light of Christ shines from His Church to distribute Our love.

Daughter, stay close to your Mother and pray always with her. Bear witness by your love because by the word of your testimony and the Blood of the Lamb, the Enemy is defeated. I bless you in the name of the Most Holy Trinity. I love you, The Eternal Father.

✝

April 16, 2004 Friday of the Octave of Easter
The Stone Rejected By the Builders

The Eternal Father began, Daughter, come, listen and write. He is the stone rejected by the builders, which has become the cornerstone. He was crucified but I raised Him from the dead and there is no other name under heaven given to the human race by which you are to be saved. He is the cornerstone of your salvation. He was raised up on the Cross to span earth to heaven to draw all things unto Him. Now He sits at My Right Hand and dominion is given to Him. Rejected once, He is exalted forever.

Today also the builders reject Him and attempt to refashion His Mystical Body according to modern values stripped of the demands of Divine Love. Christ's Mystical Body was instituted in the order of divine charity and given a living heart, the Eucharistic Heart of Jesus, and a living breath, the Holy Spirit. The Church is a living organism, a family of men, women and children, made in the image and likeness of the Creator.

The Eucharistic Heart of Jesus is the same yesterday, today and forever and the Church draws its life from the Blessed Sacrament. This is central to the life of the Church. Yet today there are some in authority who would diminish the August Sacrament of its sacrificial essence. When Jesus said to the apostles, "Do this is remembrance of Me," He not only refers to the actual transubstantiation of bread and wine into His Body and Blood but also to His own consecrated victim-hood; the laying down of His life for His friends to become the Bread of Life, nourishment for the soul of the Church. The Eucharistic Table remains an altar of sacrifice for the Lamb. The Sacrament of Love is life for the souls of the faithful.

There is division in the hierarchy and the members of the Church suffer polarization. The unity that comes from the Holy Spirit is lacking because cooperation is needed to preserve truth and unity, cooperation with the Holy Spirit. Some in authority are making decisions without seeking the counsel of the Holy Spirit, without concern for the Divine Will. The Mystical Body suffers a lack of charity and unity as the demands of the Gospel are emptied to compensate for the scandalous behavior of some in authority who betrayed the Head and Body of the Church. But the stone that is rejected remains the cornerstone and the building that is the Church shall stand amidst the fiery ordeal all around her.

You shall come to understand the sacrificial essence of charity, the virtue that crowns all others and remains forever. Divine Love is freely given but it demands a reciprocal charity requiring the free gift of self. There are few who make such a total commitment to My Son. There are many with one foot in each camp who never commit but remain undecided. This is an offense to Me and a grave danger for the soul who persists in indecision or remains lukewarm. The stone that the builders rejected has become the cornerstone of the Church that is indestructible as He is Head of the Church until the end of time. He is rejected in the human heart that makes no room for Him. Many remain indifferent to His voice, hardened to His call, preferring self-love to the perfect charity of His Sacred Heart.

He came to start a fire that would ignite the nations and that fire can not be extinguished. It is the fire of the Holy Spirit that purifies to sanctify you. The Holy Spirit begets new life for the Church and by the breath of the Spirit the sanctification of the human family is always taking place. There will come an age of sanctification, a time in human history when the Holy Spirit will illumine your understanding in such a way that scales fall from your eyes so He will be more fully known and loved. Then you will come to new life in the Divine Will to live in the love of God. (There was a pause here. Then He continued to guide my soul because I was in turmoil.)

The Dark Night

Daughter, you please Me in your service to the Mystical Body and your suffering is not in vain. Your soul has endured terrible desolation in these days following Easter. Your Beloved hides Himself. Darkness descends upon your soul. Consolation gives way to doubt as you endure a night that tries your soul forcing you to make persistent acts of faith to combat the terror of this darkness. It is permitted that your faith be tested to strengthen your will and enlarge your heart for more perfect love. Persevere to do as I ask trusting that you are not deceived but growing in grace. You are plunged now into the unity and life of the Thrice Holy One in a new grace that takes you deeper into the heart of the Trinity though you perceive yourself falling into an abyss of nothingness. Surrender unto the work of divine grace in your soul. You are never alone and your sacrifice draws grace upon your family and Church, especially the priesthood. You are my fruitful daughter under My paternal protection. Persevere to carry your cross daily. I love you, The Eternal Father.

My Response and Prayer

Abba, I am humbled to be in your service but you see how weak and weary I have become. It seems I have entered a dark, cold cave and cannot find the light of day or warm myself by any fire. My experience is one of exile. I go through the motions faithfully but you see that my heart is inconsolable. Abba, you know that I love you and cherish your paternal charity and words of wisdom. I desire to be an obedient, grateful daughter, pleasing you in every way. Help me to persevere in these new graces of purification.

I renew my fiat that you may take me deeper into the Kingdom of the Divine Will at your pace and timing. O Father, be glorified in your little child. I praise you eternally. Make my life a holocaust in reparation for my sins and those of my family. Create in me a clean heart that beats only for the Most Holy Trinity. Bless me please, eternal and good Father. Amen.

✝

April 17, 2004   Saturday of the Octave of Easter
Their Unbelief: Invoke the Holy Spirit: Proclaim the Gospel

The Eternal Father began, Daughter, come, listen and write. As the Eleven were at table, He appeared to them and rebuked them for their unbelief and hardness of heart because they had not believed those who saw Him after He had been raised. He said to them, "Go into the whole world and proclaim the Gospel to every creature." (The Gospel of the day: Mark16:14.15)

Even those beloved apostles closest to Him during His public ministry were slow to believe in His resurrection so He appeared to rebuke them for their unbelief. He needed to commission them to go into the whole world and proclaim the Gospel but in the beginning His intimate friends could not fathom His glorious victory over death. He revealed Himself to them repeatedly to build up their faith, to teach them the whole meaning of His passion, death and resurrection. He opened their eyes, minds and hearts until they could not contain their zeal having seen for themselves the promised victory of their Lord. Then he commissioned them to evangelize the nations, to baptize in His Name. These ordinary men became clothed in Christ and their zeal could not be contained. They were transformed by His life and love and would bear witness to the Truth until their lives would be given up in defense of the Church.

Today also, ordinary men and women are giving up their lives in defense of the Church. These martyrs of the modern age perpetuate the sacrifice of the Lamb and are saints giving blood for the life of the Church. You have many brothers and sisters risking their lives to worship My Son, attending the Sacrifice of the Mass in secret for fear of annihilation or imprisonment. In some nations where the Church is suppressed, faith sprouts through the underground Church because a good shepherd (priest) risks all to consecrate bread and wine into the Lord's Body, Blood, Soul and Divinity to feed souls. In the midst of such oppression, people strive to transcend their existence and the Gospel attracts and brings hope. There are many living heroic lives of faith in the worst of human conditions. There are priests at risk of losing their lives in many anti-cleric countries. There are missionaries who forsake their comfortable lives to bring the Truth to people in distress.

Yours is an age of martyrs and their blood is not in vain but is becoming a river of new life for the Church. This river flows from every nation toward the Church in Rome, toward the Vicar of Christ. He sees this as a sign of something new to come and has prophesied a future civilization of love. There will be more blood shed before this prophecy is fulfilled but it shall come to pass.

There is more a crisis of faith in some nations where freedom of worship is guaranteed by law. Your nation's freedoms are guaranteed by the law of the land but are vulnerable to attacks from enemies, large and small nations, who have extreme hatred for your country. There are many enemies of the Church in your country who vehemently challenge the laws to eradicate any notion of a Supreme Being to create an atheistic nation. It shall be increasingly necessary to defend the deposit of faith as the nations unite to govern the world by man's laws and aspirations. They shall be moved to re-write your history and bury the teachings of Christ. Great will be the need to evangelize the nations who have already known the Gospel but now suppress it.

It will be necessary to suffer persecution from the world for belief in My Son so man's unbelief turns to faith. Such persecution of the Body of Christ will increase so you become like soldiers warring against seen and unseen enemies in defense of the teaching of the Church. The Spirit goes before you and prepares the faithful for all that is to come. Whoever has ears should listen to what the Spirit is saying and contemplate seriously the signs that surround you, for it is late in the day of mercy.

The Lord Jesus appeared to His apostles and rebuked them for their unbelief and hardness of heart. What shall He do for those who persist in unbelief and hardness of heart in your age? Only those who open their hearts to the Holy Spirit will persevere in spreading and living the Gospel to the end. The Holy Spirit is the vital and necessary agent of faith, hope and love. By His power there will be another fullness of Pentecost, as if tongues of fire descended anew upon His disciples. When faith in My Son appears as if lost and the Church appears as if breaking apart, remember the promise of your Eternal Father, My covenant of charity and of mercy. I desire to restore what I have created in love. I am not glorified in a dead people who have lost faith in My Son. I am not glorified in a sin-sick world. The Holy Spirit will pour out His torrent of grace, raise a pure people and make holy what I have created. The whole world should be consecrated to the Holy Spirit! But you have yet to know Him and receive Him fully. His hour is coming and I ask that you hasten to invoke His hour!

Daughter, unite your prayers to the Immaculate Heart of Mary, Mother of the Church, of all Nations, Queen of Martyrs, Refuge of Sinners and beloved spouse of the Holy Spirit. I bless you, my child. I love you, The Eternal Father.

✟

April 18, 2004   Divine Mercy Sunday
To Show Mercy

The Eternal Father began, Daughter, come, listen and write. Jesus said to them again, "Peace be with you. As the Father has sent Me, so I send you." And when He had said this, He breathed on them and said to them, "Receive the Holy Spirit. Whose sins you forgive are forgiven them and whose sins you retain are retained." (The Gospel of the day: John 20:20-25)

My beloved Son greeted them and conferred peace upon them. He begins to tell them again that He was sent by His Abba, Father. He sends them out into the world, first breathing on them, instructing them to receive the Holy Spirit.

I sent Him into the world as God-Man to reveal Mercy. The God-Man willed to suffer, die and arise again to reveal Mercy. The Descent of the Holy Spirit reveals Mercy. The greatest attribute of the Trinitarian Family is the unfathomable attribute of Divine Mercy.

I am a compassionate Father filled with tenderness toward human misery and always moving in fidelity to My word of clemency. I hear your anguished cries for help and I am moved to compassion because of the love I have for you and because of the Precious Blood that covers you. Divine justice is also a facet of divine mercy and is never without conscious goodness, freely willed. The gratuitous gift of paternal mercy none the less requires a pious response: that you receive the gift of mercy and turn to become merciful, also. The attributes of the Eternal Three are meant to become your attributes too, for you are to become like the Lord your God by virtue of your communion with My Son by the workings of the Spirit. Thus you are carried by grace into the merciful embrace of your Good Father.

Jesus tells the apostles, "Whose sins you forgive are forgiven them and whose sins you retain are retained." Thus the sacrament of reconciliation is instituted by My Son who gives authority to His consecrated priesthood for the forgiveness of sins. The priesthood of Christ is the dispenser of divine mercy. The authority to bind or loose sin is the utmost of charisms bestowed upon priests originating from the pierced Heart of the Redeemer. Many priests forget the importance of this neglected Sacrament because they too, have been lulled to sleep regarding sin. If the faithful are not reminded about this Sacrament, then few are drawn to come to the fount of mercy to be healed. This is suffocating the distribution of Divine Mercy. I desire the administration of justice be crowned with "tender love" so that by My merciful example, slowly, the human heart is enlarged to the dimensions of the Heart of God.

Sin is a personal responsibility though it affects the universal dehumanization of the human family. The humble ones have discovered the fount of Divine Mercy in the sacrament of reconciliation and avail themselves of its restorative, healing power. Divine Charity is most fully expressed in the seven sacramental fountains of the Church. Divine Mercy is most fully expressed in the sacrament for forgiveness of sins.

Great is the need for repentance of sin in this, your age of mediocrity and faithlessness. Now there is more deadness due to sin, more indifference to sin, more selfishness and moral perversion due to sin, more excuses for sin, more opportunities for sin, more isolation, death and suffering due to sin. It is as if the whole of creation has advanced in the ways of the Evil One and become hardened to sin and indifferent to responsibility to the law of divine charity. Our Commandments are viewed as confinement of freedom, rather than the key to authentic freedom.

Do you not realize that your Father has a heart that characterizes divine mercy? I beckon the world to turn in repentance and with trust to The Divine Mercy. This requires a new personal and universal awareness of sin in the world, a new desire to oppose what is sinful in favor of what is altogether good. This requires the right judgment of a well formed conscience together with the active pursuit of what is Godly. The Kingdom of the Divine Will calls humanity away from sin and beckons to the greater good, the way of holiness, the way of filial mercy and reconciliation.

The smokescreen of the Evil One hides the true motive which is entrapment to sin and death. Convinced that Satan is not a reality, that hell does not exist, that sin is an illusion, the person goes the way of selfish, sensual love to live a lie. Mired in sickness of soul, such a person fails to discover the true beauty and meaning of a life lived in communion with the Most Holy Trinity. While Satan tempts you to a lifestyle of sin only to entrap you to slavish desires, the Holy Spirit counsels you to resist temptation, and remain true to your heavenly Father.

The Holy Spirit instructs your conscience to know right from wrong. He is called the Teacher, Counselor, Sanctifier and your Advocate, who consecrates you in the Truth. You must open the door to your heart, the door to your free-will, to receive His sanctifying presence. Desire on your part is necessary, because the Holy Spirit will not violate your free will and awaits your cooperation. My Beloved Son instructs you as He instructed His apostles, "Receive the Holy Spirit." Let Him breathe upon you now.

See how every word from the mouth of My Beloved Son is pregnant with meaning and pertinent in every age for the life of grace. The Most Holy Trinity is perpetually alive in creation. Trinitarian mercy radiates new life for those who desire to mirror divine goodness. The kingdom of the Divine Will is fruitful mercy.

The Octave of Easter is celebrated as a liturgical Feast of Divine Mercy in the Universal Church. Heavens' floodgates of mercy are opened to pour out superabundant grace for the world. Let the message of Divine Mercy resound throughout the nations to every man, woman and child. I desire the revelation of mercy so that you may drink deeply of Divine Love and know that I am your merciful Father. I invite you, dear prodigal children, to the fount of mercy to become fully alive in Me. Creation, be reconciled to your Creator and live the Divine Will on earth as in heaven. You shall be sanctified by My Spirit and know that God is love. You are the target of Divine Mercy. Know that those who please Me are not the self-righteous but the repentant sinners. Come humbly unto your Eternal Father.

Daughter, thank you for your fidelity to Me: receive My blessing. What you are doing can be characterized as an act of filial mercy and obedience to My will. I bless you in the name of the Most Holy Trinity. I love you, The Eternal Father.

April 21, 2004
I So Loved the World

The Eternal Father began, Daughter, come, listen and write."
"I so loved the world that I gave My only begotten Son, so that whoever believes in Him might not perish but might have eternal life." (The Gospel of the day: John 3:16)
My divine charity is manifested in the gift of the Incarnation as He was sent from My merciful bosom on mission to redeem fallen humanity. I sent My only begotten Son into the world and no human mind can grasp the profundity of My Gift. If you believe in Him, then you believe in Me for He is My face and heart for you. In seeing Him, you see Me, for we are two persons in one bond of inexpressible love. He came that you might have eternal life, therefore when I behold Our prodigal children, every nation under the heavens, I see Him, His Blood as a blanket over creation covering your sinfulness with perfect innocence. Beyond your grasp, I know what He suffered for love of you. Through Him, I covered you with divine mercy to rescue you from eminent, eternal separation from the Thrice Holy One.

Let your hearts rejoice and overflow with gratitude at the revelation of Divine Love. It is for each person, an individual, personalized gift, a covenant of charity that promises a future of eternal glory in the Triune Godhead. Paternal omnipotence is manifested from the beginning as My divine initiatives brought forth creation, salvation and sanctification. Is there another before I AM?

Your dignity is found in My love as you are created in the image and likeness of your God, Uncreated and Supreme Being. My sovereignty is over all created things and though some have wandered far from Me, I do not banish you to exile but reach for you always and everywhere.

Many people rebel against Divine Love modeling the fallen Lucifer who refused Me obedience, desiring to have glory for himself. I willed The Garden of Eden but Adam and Eve fell to the temptation of the Ancient Serpent. In the fullness of time, the New Adam, the Christ and the New Eve, the Immaculate Conception, came to restore what was lost and lead you back into the garden of The Tree of Life. It can be understood that your soul experiences the Garden of Eden, the communion of creature with Creator, in the power of the Holy Spirit, through grace won for you through the Cross.

Your communion with Me is the fruit of a sacramental life modeled in the beatitudes, lived in childlike docility to the Holy Spirit. Our communion is realized by the desire of your heart and the yielding of your free will to the Divine Will. Faith, hope and love in the soul form a river of grace and this waters the heart to produce the good fruit of the Spirit. The image of My Son is then reproduced in your soul and I am glorified.

There are many who persist in selfishness due to pride and this is a destructive force in the human family. He came as the Light of the world but men preferred the darkness and to His own He revealed divine love but they did not accept Him. Heaven bends to earth and extends every necessary grace but Darkness has its hour and claims many souls. The lambs who know His voice remain near Him while the goats wander far from the Good Shepherd.

The earth is full of deception at this hour and I am made to observe much suffering from sin and lack of faith, hope and love. The world would self destruct if not for manifold divine graces distributed through the maternal mediation of the Mother of God. The Spirit of the Living God will again manifest to restore and sanctify creation. Can the Heavenly Jerusalem come down except from Above? Invoke the Holy Spirit toward a New Pentecost so many will come back to the paternal embrace and friendship of the Trinity. In this manner, I will be glorified and you shall receive the inheritance won for you by the Perfect Sacrifice of the Lamb.

The Holy Spirit will teach you how to return the love that has been poured into your heart. Then you shall not be lost for lack of repentance. The gift of God shall be received by humanity as intended from the dawn of ages. I so loved the world and all that is in it, to excess. I expressed this in a manner which nothing can surpass in the gift of My beloved Son. He came to make you understand the ardent appeal of Divine Love. In the perfect unity of the Divine Will, He is the obedient Son. To the degree that you become like Him, you know My perpetual affection as your Father.

On the Cross, Love reveals in a decisive way Its intensity and that is why you are sealed in the sign of the Cross, baptized into His death and receive new life in Him. Take up your Cross daily and follow His footsteps to Calvary's Summit, becoming one with Him. Then I will be glorified in you, as I am in Him and you will have life in Me and know the love of your Father.

Daughter, persevere to record the graces in your soul. I bless you in the name of the Most Holy Trinity. I love you, The Eternal Father.

April 22, 2004
God Is Trustworthy

The Eternal Father began, Daughter, Come, listen and write. The one who comes from above is above all. The one who is of the earth is earthly and speaks of earthly things. But the one who comes from heaven is above all. He testifies to what he has seen and heard, but no one accepts his testimony. Whoever does accept his testimony certifies that God is trustworthy." (The Gospel of the day: John 3:31-35)

My Beloved Son testifies to what He has seen and heard from Above because He comes from Above and there is no other who has come down from Above to testify as He does. He tells you what He has seen and knows so that you believe in His word and know the reason for your faith in Him.

Your existence has meaning that is fully revealed in the Word Incarnate. He is the Truth and He bears witness to Me so that you may believe and have eternal life. His testimony is altogether trustworthy because God is true and cannot lie. Let this be your consolation and the guiding light that illumines your path to Paradise. You are on a journey to your eternal reward and My Son Jesus has gone before you to prepare a place for you. I have already set a heavenly banquet for those who believe in Him and persevere to the end.

Let your faith in Him enkindle a living charity in your heart and move you to respond in hope. Your earthly exile is but a blink of an eye; a passage toward eternal life in communion with your Creator. How do you reciprocate to the tender mercies of your Triune God?

For a moment you consider the truth of Divine Love but quickly you are allured away from spiritual realities for base, tangible things that capture your heart away from Me. For all your infidelities, I do not reject you but wait patiently upon your repentance. What is time to Me? I am outside of time, yet for everything there is an appointed hour so the divine plan and promise presses forward and it shall not be late. I will not condemn you; rather, you will convict yourself in the light of Truth when you see yourself as you really are: naked for lack of repentance of sin. I await one glance from you toward Me. If I see one small movement of your heart toward Me, one hand outstretched toward heaven, I bend to meet you, to pick you up and place you back on the straight and narrow path to heaven.

The virtues of faith, hope and love in your soul are the arms that reach for Me as I bend to you. These three virtues unite us and forge a bond of abiding love. Do you think that I desire My children to be paralyzed by fear and burdened with sadness? I sent Him to set you free from fear of death and condemnation. I sent Him to ransom you and He has relieved your burden and restored your freedom as children of God. I am a merciful, sovereign Father yet I bend for you because of the love I have for you as I behold you in My Mind's Eye in the perfected state of grace and am well pleased with the result brought about by My grace. I reach for you through My Only Begotten Son. Follow His footsteps to come to Me as He is the Way and the Door to my heart. He certifies the trustworthiness of the Almighty One. Trust in Me and let faith be the vehicle that raises you up to the heights of Love. By trust in Me, you will soar like the eagle. By fear you never reach the goal. Better to trust in Me so that you have your being in the Most Holy Trinity and live in peace.

Daughter, I bless and thank you for your surrender unto the Divine Will.

I love you, The Eternal Father.

✝

April 24, 2004
Do Not Be Afraid

The Eternal Father began, Daughter, come, listen and write. When they had rowed three or four miles, they saw Jesus walking on the sea and coming near the boat, and they began to be afraid. But He said to them, "It is I. Do not be afraid." (The Gospel of the day: John 6:19-20)

Jesus reveals Himself to the beloved apostles with the words, "It is I. Do not be afraid." He says, "Do not be afraid" because fear is a great obstacle to faith in Him. These words of the Lord are not only for the apostles who saw Him walking on the water approaching their boat though they experienced an imposing, extraordinary phenomenon that rendered them afraid at the awareness of His omnipotence. His words resound in a personal manner for every believer because they originate from the compassionate Heart of the Redeemer who identifies with the human condition, so prone to fear from lack of faith.

He extends His Heart as a bridge from fear to trust and is constant in telling you, His dearly beloved brothers and sisters: "It is I; here I am, recognize Me!" My Son draws close because intimacy with Him moves you from the paralysis of fear to the liveliness of faith. I have referred to His Heart as the bridge because His Heart encompassed Calvary's Cross and it can be understood that His Heart and the Cross are integrated to form the bridge to cross from death to life.

In the wake of His passion, death and resurrection, there was trembling and disbelief, fear of persecution and fear of My Son. His words to the apostles become a testimony and consolation. Throughout the ages they became a revelation of the tender mercy of the Redeemer who approaches mankind with consistent invitation to come unto Him as His Heart is always open. He makes Himself approachable because of His patient humility and excess charity. He who is the perfect Love goes out of Himself because it is His nature to extend Himself to beget communion with the object of His affection. Communion is the point of Love's constant action. The greatest obstacle to communion is fear; fear of the unknown, fear of the unseen, fear of condemnation, fear of vulnerability, fear of losing oneself to another.

When the Lord of the Universe approaches His creatures with the reassurance of His Presence, He is again making Himself vulnerable to humanity in order to draw all things unto Himself so that by means of the Bridge, you may come to know the incomprehensible joy of communion with the Redeemer who brings you to Me.

The revelation of Divine Love is complete in the Person of the Word Incarnate but personal cooperation is still being realized until the end of time when the world as you know it will change and the final judgment will separate the sheep from the goats. The final destination of every man, woman and child will be realized at a time known only to Me.

Unholy fear paralyzes your age. Do not be afraid, My prodigal children! Be amazed by paternal mercy. Be grateful for your Redeemer. Let the Holy Spirit change unholy fear to the proper Fear of the Lord, so that on earth you experience already a communion of friendship in the mutual gift of yourself; you to My Son and My Son to you. Then when you witness the stupendous power of the Lord, you will respond in holy amazement, be moved by Charity and filled with gratitude. Do not be afraid to draw close the Heart of the Redeemer. It is there that you will find rest, strength and perseverance in all life's trying moments. Christ is always identifying Himself for love of you and in the most distressing people and places you will find Him manifesting His omnipotence in extraordinary ways to draw you deeper into faith. If you must meet Him in fear, let it be reverential fear that shows itself in adoration of the Beloved.

Your faith must be strengthened to undergo the test and purification necessary toward the kingdom of the Divine Will on earth. In every nation and among all people, the Holy Spirit is manifesting signs and wonders to strengthen faith, hope and love. There is nothing to fear except eternal separation from your Creator for whom you are made. By your communion with My Son, your focus on Him, your will reap the fruits of eternal salvation. In your unity with Him, there can be no fear because His perfect love casts out all fear.

Daughter, let the Holy Spirit continue to guide your prayers and with docility respond to the movements of divine grace in your soul. I bless you in the name of the Most Holy Trinity. I love you, The Eternal Father.

✝

May 30, 2004, Solemnity of Pentecost
In the Upper Room: A New Pentecost

The Eternal Father began, Daughter, come, listen and write. Jesus said to his disciples: "If you love me, you will keep my commandments. And I will ask the Father, and he will give you another Advocate to be with you always. Whoever loves me will keep my word, and my Father will love him, and we will come to him and make our dwelling with him. Those who do not love me do not keep my words; yet the word you hear is not Mine but that of the Father who sent me. I have told you this while I am with you. The Advocate, The Holy Spirit whom the Father will send in my name, will teach you everything and remind you of all that I told you." (The Gospel of the day: John 14:15-16, 23b-26)

This day the Universal Church celebrates the solemnity of Pentecost, the hour when the Christian faith was born by the coming of the Holy Spirit who is Divine Person, Spirit, and Breath proceeding from the unity of Perfect Charity: Father and Son.

When the Holy Spirit descended upon the Apostles and those gathered around Mary Immaculate in the Upper Room, it can be understood that My covenant of divine charity is made fruitful beyond expectation. The Spirit descended upon those gathered in prayer who were doing as Jesus told them, awaiting the promised Advocate of Whom Jesus told them.

The Spirit descended from heaven as tongues of fire and the power of the Most High manifested in the souls of each person awaiting Him. They were re-created by the transforming power of the Holy Spirit. They were given wisdom, knowledge and understanding of the ways of Divine Love. Mysteries of the Life of Christ were revealed and understood by them. What the Apostles did not understand when they beheld Jesus in the flesh, they understood now, in the coming of The Holy Spirit. The weak were made strong and fear was banished from their hearts. They were clothed with power from Above and consecrated in the truth of gospel. Only now could they bear witness to what they had seen in the public life of Christ as His constant companions.

My Only Begotten Son is the fulfillment of My covenant to send a Messiah to redeem fallen humanity. The Descent of the Holy Spirit at Pentecost is the fulfillment of My promise to make fruitful His Saving Act unto the ends of the earth, unto the end of time. This is realized by the coming of the Spirit of Truth who ratifies what Jesus told you, who perpetually consecrates you in the Truth so you are led by the same Spirit that led the God-man in His mission of salvation. The Holy Spirit sanctifies humanity by the unction of His Presence in you.

You have yet to understand the Holy Spirit is the outcry of the Heart of the Redeemer, the fruitfulness of His prayer to Me. He prayed to His Father, asking that you would be one with Us as We are One ineffable reality of Divine Love.

The saving act of salvation was complete in the Passion, Death and Resurrection of My Son but its perpetual fruitfulness would be realized by the coming of the Holy Spirit. The Holy Spirit makes His Perfect Sacrifice fruitful and personal in the individual souls of the human family as you are His temples, where He dwells to remind you of what Jesus said and did for you.

The Holy Spirit rejoices in one thing only, the Second Person of the Holy Trinity. The Spirit glories in the Fruit of the Womb of the Immaculate Conception. Jesus is always and only, born of the Holy Spirit and this is why there could be no Church, no fruit of Divine Charity, without the person of the Holy Spirit. I, the Eternal Father engendered in my Bosom, the Church, but the Holy Spirit formed the Church on earth upon the foundation of Christ Crucified and Resurrected.

The Divine Will is the transformation of each person into the ideal of divine charity, the Person of My Son Jesus. But this is only realized through the Person of the Holy Spirit whose role it is to conceive Jesus in the souls of the human family to make fruitful Divine Charity.

He is the sanctifier of the Church, of each member, as He infuses Divine Love throughout the Mystical Body. He is the unifier of the redeemed, unifying the Head and the Body of the Church, imprinting Christ's image upon the souls of the faithful and infusing ineffable Divine Charity into all that is meant to give glory to The Holy Trinity. The Holy Spirit excels in creating the basis of love in the Church and this Perfect Charity is unique in its fruitfulness. The Spirit perpetuates more love for the glory of the Son.

The Holy Spirit is unique in His power to disarm the Enemy who is always and forever defeated by the power of Divine Love. Are you beginning to understand the exalted nature of the workings of the Holy Spirit? The faithful have yet to appreciate the sending forth of the Spirit. Jesus ardently desired to pour out the Love of the Trinity through the Person of the Holy Spirit.

The sublime and divine mission of the Holy Spirit is one of transformation into Christ, the sanctification of the human race, from beginning to end, so that the Church militant is prepared to become the Church triumphant. This is Love's divine initiative and the Spirit is well equipped with every necessary gift to bring to life that which is dead, to make holy that which is sinful, and to transform you, My people, into a holy nation by virtue of the Divine Guest of your soul.

Oh! That you would be transformed into Love and become My Son's mirror image by the powerful dynamism of the Holy Spirit! Oh! That the Spirit of Truth would triumph in your souls so that you become credible witnesses to the transforming power of the Holy Spirit! Then the world would see Christ in all His glory, present on earth through you, Church alive!

The Holy Spirit seeks after souls to pour out His infinite treasures: human temples in which He can create a holy environment of communion. He is the Gift of God with infinite capacity to renew you, individually and communally. The whole of the universe is in need of His transforming charity to come to life, to resurrect, so to be led by Him into the Garden of Eden restored. He is the divine architect of the kingdom of the Divine Will, the restorer of what is lost, the re-builder of the City of God.

Invoke the Holy Spirit so that your stony hearts become fleshy, responsive to the life of Christ within you. Invoke His Holy Name upon yourself and those you love. Invoke Him more fully in the Church so to be led by Him in all your ways of worship and praise. Consecrate yourselves to His Holy Love and become apostles of the Holy Spirit.

His hour is coming: the hour when you will experience Him as in the Upper Room, as in a personal Pentecost. The Spirit's hour will be the reign of Sacred Heart of Jesus. Receive the Spirit of Love, who proceeds from the Me and from The Son, who has been poured into your hearts by the most charitable act of the Divine Will. Only through Him will you give your fiat to the Divine Will and live. I love you, The Eternal Father.

Prayer for Pentecost
Veni, Sancte Spiritus

Come, Holy Spirit, come!
And from your celestial home
  Shed a ray of light divine!
Come, Father of the poor!
Come, source of all our store!
  Come, within our bosoms shine.
You, of comforters the best;
You, the soul's most welcome guest;
  Sweet refreshment here below;
In our labor, rest most sweet;
Grateful coolness in the heat;
  Solace in the midst of woe.
O most blessed Light divine,
Shine within these hearts of yours,
  And our inmost being fill!
Where you are not, we have naught,
Nothing good in deed or thought,
  Nothing free from taint of ill.
Heal our wounds, our strength renew;
On our dryness pour your dew;
  Wash the stains of guilt away:
Bend the stubborn heart and will;
Melt the frozen, warm the chill;
  Guide the steps that go astray.
On the faithful, who adore
And confess you, evermore
  In your sevenfold gift descend;
Give them virtue's sure reward;
Give them your salvation, Lord;
  Give them joys that never end. Amen.
Alleluia.

June 6, 2004   Solemnity of the Most Holy Trinity
The Trinitarian Family

After Holy Communion, The Eternal Father began, Daughter, come, listen and write. Jesus said to his disciples: "I have much more to tell you, but you cannot bear it now. But when he comes, the Spirit of truth, he will guide you to all truth. He will not speak on his own, but he will speak what he hears, and will declare to you the things that are coming. He will glorify me, because he will take from what is mine and declare it to you." (The Gospel of the day: John 16:12-14)

I, The Eternal Father, grant special graces to coincide with the Church's solemnity honoring Three Persons in One. The Holy Spirit has declared the truth and revealed the Godhead. The Word Incarnate revealed Himself as the only Son of His Father. The unity of Three Persons in One God is an incomprehensible mystery to mankind, outside human understanding because of the duality in the human person. God alone possess perfect unity. While you strive for this ideal it is accomplished only by the power of the Holy Spirit that carries you into the family unity of the Father, Son and Holy Spirit.

Three Persons of the Blessed Trinity are ever mindful of you because we are a family of Love giving new life to perpetuate our communion with you. I speak to you as a patient, merciful Father who loves what is created by the Divine Will. You have been carried to the family of the Trinity that you may bring glory to My kingdom and become perfected in grace.

There is no brotherhood on earth without the knowledge of your Eternal Father. As the Father of a spiritual race, I gather you together as a true family. My divine paternity is manifested in the person of Jesus, sent to earth to generate spiritual offspring by the powerful dynamism of the Spirit. He made you adopted sons and daughters by His passion, death and resurrection. In Him, your communion with the family of the Holy Trinity is realized.

The Spirit of Love directs the Church to generate new life. The history of humanity is unfolding through the drama of each person's life. Your individual and collective journey back to the bosom of your Father is made in the presence of all Three Persons of the Trinity. It is impossible that you can be alone on the journey because each person is ever present in My Mind's eye. I know and love everything that has come into existence in the Divine Will. That which is created in love is sustained by love and drawn back to the Origin. Love originates and returns to Three Persons: Father, Son and Holy Spirit.

As Father, I have shown the immensity of My tender mercy in loving and forgiving you. I seek a community of little ones, children to whom I can reveal the splendor of Divine Mercy. That you would love as I have loved you and forgive as I forgive you is what I ask. That you would reflect My mercy toward one another is a sign that you come from Me. That you would seek after My Son and honor Him, is how you best glorify Me.

You know Me as Father through My Son and you know Jesus by the revelation of the Holy Spirit who speaks only of Him. You know the family of the Trinity by faith. Your faith is expressed by bearing witness to what you know: that you believe and have hope in all three persons of the Trinity. The sum of the Blessed Trinity is Love. The sum of creation must become reciprocal love so that the unity of Creator with creature is complete. The perfection of Divine Love is expressed in the divine family. You also are perfected in relationship to a human family in which you are all brothers and sisters in Christ. Strive for unity and love as you make your way back to Me. Come to know yourselves as the children of a merciful Father. You are drawn into the Holy Trinity when you are baptized into the family of Divine Love.

My child, I bless you in the name of the Most Holy Trinity. Thank you for your obedience and courage in carrying the Cross. I love you, The Eternal Father.

June 13, 2004
Solemnity of the Most Holy Body & Blood of Christ
Eucharist: Bread that Comes Down from Heaven

The Eternal Father began, Daughter, come, listen and write. Jesus said, "Whoever believes has eternal life. Your ancestors ate the manna in the desert, but they died; this is the bread that comes down from heaven so that one may eat it and not die. I am the living bread that came down from heaven; whoever eats this bread will live forever; and the bread that I will give is my flesh for the life of the world." (John 6:47-51)

Today the Church observes the Solemnity of the Most Holy Body and Blood of Christ. My Beloved Son feeds the multitudes and whoever eats worthily of His Body, Blood, Soul and Divinity partakes in the banquet of divine love to the glory of the Trinity. The Church points the faithful to the Eucharistic Banquet that is the summit of what you believe. The Truth proclaimed in the Gospel is handed down through the apostolic priesthood of Christ. This divine mystery is incomprehensible to the natural man but to the spiritual man it is a matter of faith, a matter of experiential love: a communion.

My Son remains with you, the Church on earth, in the humble species of bread and wine become His Body and Blood for the life of each soul and he who worthily partakes of the Eucharist is changed according to the state of his soul and faith in his heart. Creator and creature commune in his heavenly banquet because the priest of the new and eternal covenant offered the Perfect Sacrifice on the Cross. This sacrifice is perpetuated through the consecrated hands of the priests who offer the Holy Sacrifice of the Mass throughout the world to feed the faithful the Bread of Life. This imperishable Bread is the Risen Heart of the Redeemer that unites His soul to yours to communicate the love of the Most Holy Trinity. The Eucharist is the heart of the Church that pumps the life blood throughout the Body to transfigure you. For what is imperfect is being perfected by sacramental grace.

The Eucharist draws the faithful toward the Light and strengthens each person for the rigors of walking the straight and narrow path that is the Gospel of Jesus. The Church fulfills her duty to renew the faithful by the power of the Eucharist and this is why Christ's Vicar, Pope John Paul II, has proclaimed a year of the Eucharist. The Church continues to invite the faithful to return to the Source of Life for the sake of restoring faith, hope and love. In the midst of a crisis of faith, of waning hope and lack of charity in homes, nations, the Church and world, the Eucharist is elevated to draw all peoples back to Christ.

In the Eucharist you have the remedy for what ails mankind and by means of the Eucharistic Heart of Jesus the nations will come to know that God exists because many nations who once believed, have now forsaken the faith that anchored them in Me.

Pray for the unification of Church through the power of the Eucharist. This sacrament has the power to effect great change for good in the Church and world. What begins in the soul of each individual radiates through the Church and world. Pray that many will return to the state of grace and begin anew to partake in the Eucharistic Life of the Church. It is by this means that the peace of the world will be established. This will happen through the maternal mediation of the Blessed Virgin Mary because she is Mother of the Bread come down from heaven. There are none as perfect as she, in adoration of the Blessed Sacrament!

The Immaculate Heart of Mary is Co-redemptrix, Mediatrix and Advocate for all peoples and the vessel through whom many will return to the Eucharistic Table. A Mother perfected in grace leads her children to the best nourishment knowing what is necessary to the life of each soul. This most charitable of Mothers and Queen of Heaven is the Mother of the Eucharist who knows well how to lead her wayward children back to the source of new life for their souls. She mediated the establishment of the early Church and continues throughout history, to mediate the establishment of the kingdom of the Divine Will.

Daughter, you draw life from the Eucharist daily. Continue to live fully the Eucharistic charity that brings you to the heart of the

Trinity. Pray in reparation for the offenses against the Eucharist as daily I am made to observe countless atrocities in the unworthy reception of the Most August Sacrament. There are many who believe that the Eucharist is a symbol only. This grieves heaven, wounds the Mystical Body and profanes His Holy Name. Continue to intercede for the conversion of all souls by the power of the Eucharist. I bless you in the name of the Most Holy Trinity. I love you, The Eternal Father."

My Response and Prayer to Make Reparation

Abba, beloved Father of the Eucharist, be glorified in my weakness. Help me to do as you ask: make reparation to appease divine justice and draw mercy upon those who offend Your Perfect Charity by receiving the Eucharist without proper disposition.

Father, all men sin and are unworthy to receive Your Son in the Eucharist but at each Mass we pray, "Only say the word and we shall be healed". By means of the Eucharistic Heart of Jesus grant the Church and world be purified for the sake of the Precious Blood that gushed from His pierced side for the salvation of sinners. As we drink the Cup may we become one with the Heart of the Redeemer who glorifies you, His Beloved Father.

Jesus said, "Behold I make all things new." Regenerate His life and love throughout the Mystical Body, in all souls, so that the prayer He taught, "Give us this day, our daily bread," is realized physically and spiritually by means of a Holy Communion.

May souls receive the grace of conversion and the Church be restored fully by means of the inexhaustible fountain of His Eucharistic and Priestly Heart. Abba, Hallowed be Thy Name on earth as in heaven by means of a Eucharistic people who worship you in Spirit and in Truth. Amen.

✝

June 18, 2004 Solemnity of the Sacred Heart
For Priests: The Heart of the Redeemer

The Eternal Father began: Daughter, come, listen and write. Jesus addressed this parable to the Pharisees and scribes: What man among you having a hundred sheep and losing one of them would not leave the ninety-nine in the desert and go after the lost one until he finds it. And when he does find it he sets it on his shoulders with great joy and upon his arrival home, he calls together his friends and neighbors and says to them, "Rejoice with me because I have found my lost sheep." I tell you in just the same way there will be more joy in heaven over one sinner who repents than over ninety-nine righteous people who have no need of repentance." (Gospel of the day: Luke 15:3-7)

Jesus speaks a revelation of Trinitarian mercy portraying our joy in receiving a repentant sinner, into the embrace of our love. My Son, Eternal Word Made Flesh, is sent to earth to envelop creation in the incomprehensible mercy of the Eternal Godhead. The mission of the Redeemer is the reconciliation of creation to Creator through the greatest act of divine mercy. The Pierced Heart of the Redeemer is that sacred organ signifying His infinite mercy. My beloved Son is The Divine Mercy.

The Sacred Heart of Jesus, so violently pierced on Calvary's Mount, gushed saving blood and living water to bathe creation in divine mercy. He was sent and to His own He came but they did not receive Him yet He loved them. When he had suffered, died and arose again, when He ascended to my right hand, the Holy Spirit descended upon the Church at Pentecost to empower the early Church to give witnesses to His merciful act of Salvation. From the Upper Room the name and mission of the Redeemer would be carried as the Holy Spirit proclaimed and consecrated the Church in the truth. The parables of My beloved Son were told and received as the Good News because the mercy of the Almighty One touched their hearts.

Today the Church worships the Most Sacred Heart of Jesus giving honor to the priestly Heart of the Good Shepherd and Victim Lamb who was pierced for love of sinners. There are manifold graces today for the Church and world issuing from the Sacred Heart of the Redeemer. My Beloved Son searches the earth to find a resting place in the human heart. Whoever opens his heart receives My Son and is graced in His friendship and Lordship.

The Sacred Heart of My Son extends an invitation to all, "Come and approach Me! Do not fear to draw close. My heart is broken open so you may enter." His Heart is ablaze with divine love and mercy. He is compelled to impart His holy zeal to the soul who is unafraid to receive Him. The Sacred Heart of Jesus is His priceless gift to humanity, a realm of pure light, a castle with countless chambers and infinite riches. Each royal chamber is the perfect environment for a delectable banquet where you are fed rich fare by His gentle hand and warmed in the radiance of His majestic beauty. So that your heart may radiate His Own, consecrate yourselves to the Sacred Heart so that by means of your entrustment to Him, He possesses you fully because you have surrendered to Him. In this way your heart will enlarge like His and you will be a vessel of mercy like Him and this is how you give glory to Me.

For The Priests

On this day of special blessing for the Church, the Sacred Heart seeks to draw close to the consecrated brotherhood of priests to restore you. For in your day, some have fallen and tarnished the good name of His priestly succession. Jesus desires to see His priesthood alive with charity for He has reserved singular graces for His chosen brotherhood so you become mirrors of His Heart. It is your heart that he seeks after because it is the place of intimacy. The One Eternal High Priest longs to draw you into divine intimacy to bestow upon you, His gift of mercy. He seeks to give you hope in this day when you walk in the shadow of a dark night for the priesthood. I, your merciful Father behold the movements of your heart and provide what you need to become like Jesus. Do not lose faith in this trying hour but redouble your commitment to

Him and watch what I do to restore what was lost, to improve your rank and invigorate your brotherhood.

The consecrated soul of the priest is meant to be that catalyst of Divine Love igniting the world in faith and hope. The truth of divine love must be proclaimed from clean lips that speak from a pure heart conformed to Christ Crucified as these are the only credible witnesses. The Sacred Heart of My Son is extended outward, ready to be placed inside the bosom of each priest so through you, souls may draw life. The soul of the priest is to be food for the faithful. And you are fed from Christ's priesthood. Since Christ lives eternally, priesthood is unchanged. (He 7:24) Yet left to himself, man is incapable of holiness. Therefore, it is from Christ Himself that the perfect priesthood is realized and hoped for. The priesthood is rooted in the very core of His Sacred Heart that loves perfectly, perpetually and infinitely. By His art of divine charity, the priesthood is being perfected by grace.

The priest who scandalizes the little ones is cut off from the Vine as dead branches that bear no good fruit are separated out and die. But the sin that encroaches upon the priesthood is the sin of the world so the entire Body of Christ, all who are baptized, priest, prophet and king, are responsible for the lack of holiness. Reparation is needed to correct the ailing parts of the Mystical Body. Let the priests receive the first fruits of your sacrificial prayer and suffering so in turn, they may become the healers and repairers of the breach.

Write This:

The Sacred Heart of Jesus is My most treasured gift to humanity. It is a priestly heart that offers sacrifice to save all men. The love between the First and Second Person of the Most Holy Trinity is inexpressible in any language and incomprehensible unto eternity. His Sacred Heart is the most adorable, obedient, docile, pure, humble and holiest of vessels to the glory of My Name. Receive His Sacred Heart into your own so you may be filled with His life of grace.

Daughter, rejoice in His gift of mercy and surrender unto the

Bridegroom. He came to ransom sinners like you. He searched and found you wandering on your own. He set you upon His shoulders and carried you to your Father's House. Let your heart be enkindled in the fire of His Love. Know that your gratitude is reparation for all those who have received mercy but do not return to thank the Lord. May gratitude form a luminous mantle around you! In this way I shall be glorified in observing my obedient and grateful daughter. May your life be one continuous hymn of praise as you live in the realm of the Spirit, in the refuge of the Sacred Heart, who carries you to My bosom. I love you, The Eternal Father.

✝

July 7, 2004
Seek the Lord

The Eternal Father began: Daughter, come, listen, and write. It is written, "Sow for yourselves justice, reap the fruit of piety; break up for yourselves a new field, for it is time to seek the Lord, till he come and rain down justice upon you." (From the first reading of the liturgy of the day: Hosea 10:12)

As the prophets of old warned the house of Israel, so the prophets of this, your age, warn the nations spreading the truth of the gospel to the four corners of the earth, echoing the message of My Son. The message of repentance, reconciliation and conversion is a perpetual cry to prepare the way of the Lord who is coming. It is time to seek the Lord, till he come and rain down justice upon you. Christ came to gather all things unto Himself as He was raised upon the Cross and in Him all things are made new. He came once and for all and still He comes by means of The Holy Spirit to illuminate your darkness, to refashion a people for Himself. The world being under the dominion of Satan for a time of testing, He comes by means of the Holy Spirit to disengage you from evil, purify your hearts, and perfect you by grace.

See that your old ways are leading nowhere good and seek My Son to break up a new field, to plant a new harvest, making fruitful a people heading toward draught and danger. I, your Eternal Father, implore you to seek after My Son with a new heart, a new fervor, that you may be saved from self destructing and come into the promised land of milk and honey by the power of the My Spirit renewing the face of the earth.

The Bridegroom calls. Where are His holy ones whose hearts belong to Him alone? The Bridegroom beckons, "Come to Me, surrender to Me, live in Me, put Me first." How many respond? But few are attentive to His Heart in the passing of the days, months and years. Do you understand now the importance of your response and how rare is the soul who perseveres to be attentive to the Bridegroom? Do you understand how rare is the heart that is undivided; set entirely upon Him for His glory? Where is the balm for the wounds inflicted upon Him by those who spurn His perpetual charity, deaf to His voice and blind to His presence? Who will be that healing salve that soothes the wounds inflicted upon His Mystical Body?

Daughter, be mindful of the Church today for The Lord's House is pillaged by those who take what is not theirs. (Possibly refers to the news of certain Dioceses declaring bankruptcy in the wake of the lawsuits from priest abuse cases?) The law of charity is just, but the law of your land is greedy against the House of God. Each man seeks his own good without qualm of conscience. Mercy is little considered.

Write this. I Am will rebuild My House! Out of the Church's poverty, sanctity will arise! Perversion will be made straight in My House. As thieves run out the back door, My Spirit enters the front door to reclaim the Sanctuary.

The Blessed Sacrament remains on the altar as the light in the darkness. The Lamb's sacrifice suffices and those who mirror the Lamb perpetuate His Sacrifice so heaven opens the floodgates of mercy to those who repent. I Am allows the Body to be tested in fire to burn away the dross and that which is destroyed is purification preparing the way for a new day. Look to the East, the sun is arising to eradicate the darkness. Your wars will last a little while longer and people will suffer.

But the Spirit comes with the olive branch and peace will arise from the rubble. The canticle of Mary, daughter of Israel, Queen mother of heaven and earth, said and it is written, "He has mercy on those who fear Him in every generation. He has shown the strength of His arm, He has scattered the proud in their thrones, and lifted up the lowly." (Mary's Magnificat: Luke 1:39)

The Holy Spirit fills and leads those who will worship Me in Spirit and in Truth. The Redeemer, Bridegroom of holy souls, gathers His beloved ones into His holy sanctuary to build up the Body again. Those who surrender unto the Divine Will become victim lambs to perpetuate His sacrifice and victory.

Daughter of the Trinity, you are recreated by the power of the Triumphant Cross. Charity solidifies your communion with the Bridegroom to make you a vessel of mercy, a sign of hope, a prophetic trumpet warning, "Prepare the way of the Lord". The bridegroom is coming! Blessed are you found waiting with oil in your lamps. Wisdom adorns you as you keep heartfelt vigil of prayer and service.

Pray much for those souls who are deaf and blind to spiritual realities. Creation cries out for help but betrays its Creator God. The prayerful sacrifice of a few will save the many. The Bride of Christ, the Church, is the City set upon a hill like a fortress that cannot be destroyed. She may be pillaged but the Hand of the Almighty has infinite power to restore her to a holy House of prayer. Daughter, let the heavens observe a column of incense arising from your intercessory heart, perfuming the air with reparation. Pray unceasingly, "Father, your will be done on earth as in heaven." Receive my paternal blessing and love, The Eternal Father.

July 8, 2004
The Kingdom of Heaven is at Hand

The Eternal Father began, Daughter, come, listen and write. Jesus said to His Apostles, "As you go, make this proclamation: The kingdom of heaven is at hand. Cure the sick, raise the dead, cleanse the lepers, and drive out demons. Without cost you have received; without cost you are to give." (The Gospel of the day: Mathew 10:7-8)

Daughter, do you understand the proclamation: "The kingdom of heaven is at hand" describes the present moment? The kingdom of heaven is life in the Most Holy Trinity and it is at hand in the person of My Son, Jesus. He remains with you, among creation in the person of the Holy Spirit. As you open your heart to the Holy Spirit, the kingdom of heaven arises within you. This is what is meant when it is written, "You are a temple of the Holy Spirit." The life of the Holy Trinity arises in the human heart and fills you with divine grace. This is the good news of salvation: Jesus has redeemed creation and the Holy Spirit sanctifies to build His temple where Trinitarian charity takes root, so the kingdom of blessedness can arise in creation.

Curing the sick, raising the dead, cleansing the lepers and driving out demons is the continuation of the mission of the Redeemer perpetuated by the power of the Spirit through temples of the Holy Spirit. These are souls whose fiat to the Divine Will allows the Sanctifier freedom to exercise His mission of transforming sinner into saint. The Holy Spirit is at work in your soul, the soul of the Church and world. The whole of creation is the target of His mission of sanctification in the holy name of the Lord, Jesus. The Holy Spirit is the Breath of The Almighty. The only Spirit that is holy, transforming and life-giving.

Jesus said to His Apostles, "Without cost you have received, without cost you are to give." Do you understand the hard-hearted cannot receive and therefore they cannot give? When humanity was in sin and worthy of condemnation, The Word became flesh and dwelt among you. He was sent not to condemn but to redeem the human family and it can be understood that salvation has come for all. But there is a key called "the human will" and each person must turn the key to open his heart to receive the good news of salvation. It is a free gift of God and so it is without cost that you have received. It is without cost that you are to give what you have received because the gift of Divine Love begets fruitfulness, and must generate more love. Love is never selfish but spends itself for the good of others and generates new life.

    Daughter, perpetuate the ministry of the Lord Jesus extending His healing touch to sin-sick souls. Jesus prayed, "Father, I do not wish to lose even one of those you have given to Me." Now He sits at My right hand in the far more excellent ministry of intercession. Now you are His instruments of divine charity, co-redeeming lost souls. The graces of the Holy Spirit in your soul make this a reality. The intercessors of the Lamb continue His mission by the power of transforming union with Him. Union with Him is the goal of discipleship and the point of all spiritual exercises.

    Allow the life of the Holy Trinity within your soul to generate new life and proclaim in the Church, the kingdom of heaven is at hand. Pray child, for the first conversion and perpetual conversion of the human family so that on earth, My Name is hallowed. Always turn the key of your human free will toward the Divine Will so that daily you sow seeds of new life as your heart gives rise to the kingdom of heaven on earth. Without cost you are to give and the more you give the more you will receive from My Paternal Charity. Glorify My Name and make known the truth of the gospel that is complete in the Person of My Son Jesus. Jesus is the way, the only way that points to Me. Christ Crucified and Risen is the door to heaven's banquet. Only those persons conformed to Christ Crucified will persevere to the end and receive the Crown, reward for the elect. Receive My paternal blessing and love. The Eternal Father.

July 15, 2004   Feast of St. Bonaventure
His Yoke is Easy: His Burden Light

The Eternal Father began, Daughter, come, listen and write. Jesus said, "Come to me, all you who labor and are burdened and I will give you rest. Take my yoke upon you and learn from me, for I am meek and humble of heart and you will find rest for yourselves; for my yoke is easy and my burden light." (Gospel of the day: Matthew 11:28-30)

Daughter, the Word Incarnate speaks a perpetual invitation for all of creation to come unto Him to receive solace from His most charitable heart. The Heart of the Redeemer is an abode of charity, pierced for love of creation. The exalted nature of the Savior was foretold by the prophets and revealed in the fullness of time through the Incarnation, yet He does not exalt Himself but humbles Himself to glorify Me, His Father and your Father. When He took up the yoke of your sin, He made your yoke light. When He said, "Learn from Me for I am meek and humble of heart," He invites you to imitate Him in the virtues of His Heart so gracious and saturated with love for Me! My Beloved Son is your blessedness and He alone is peace beyond understanding.

It is written that God is love and all things created are ordered to Divine Charity. He who receives the love the Trinity into his heart receives life giving grace to become like Christ; for you are made in the image and likeness of your Creator and for communion with Me that lasts forever. The dignity of the human person is yet to be understood on earth but you are meant to discover your identity as children of One Father in the daily sojourn of your earthly exile. You are to be about your Father's business. I look inside the temple of the Church to find the little children opening the scrolls of wisdom and ingesting the truth to become empowered by the Spirit of Love. I am in love with the little children and they are in love with Me. But the little children are few and I mean to increase your numbers for the sake of My glory.

The mission of the Redeemer won salvation for sinners as you are baptized into His death to receive resurrection. The Holy Spirit is the living dynamism of Divine Love whose action sanctifies the person. It is written that you are temples of the Holy Spirit and necessary partakers in the Divine Plan of creation, redemption and sanctification. The yoke of the Redeemer is His Passion, Death and Resurrection and it is light for you because He bore the weight of sin on His back. My Son is Lord but He did not deem equality with God but took on the form of a slave to all and therefore, you are free from slavery to sin. Your freedom is found only in Him as His Pierced Heart is both your fountain of grace and peaceful abode.

It is pride and every other capital sin that becomes a heavy yoke, makes you slaves and robs you of peace of soul. I, your merciful and good Father, observe a generation of proud, disobedient children wandering independently from Me. The meekness and humility of My Son is not found in you unless you are found in Him. These virtues are facets of a stupendous charity that is divine in nature. You cannot love as He loves unless you unite your human nature, your free will, to His divinity and allow His humanity to penetrate your heart, mind and soul. Then you will be different by the power of the Divine Live in you. You will be like Him in all facets of love and the virtues of His heart will become your own. Then you become peacefully, abundantly alive in Him. His meekness and humility are beatitudes of a living charity, necessary adornments of the garment of holiness.

He speaks of His yoke that cannot be forsaken. He said, "Take My yoke upon you". It is His loving invitation to come into His passion, death and resurrection, united in His Heart. The Redeemer is calling you to co-redeem with and in Him. He invites you to join His mission so that you are perfected in grace and give glory to Me, your heavenly Father even as He, My Only begotten Son, gives glory to Me. Incomprehensible is our bond of love and here, in that union with the all three persons of the Trinity, you will find rest. He brings you to Me, and I receive you through Him and no one comes to Me except in Him for He alone is the Door. Behold, He stands at the door of your free will and knocks. As you open the door to Him, He opens the door to Me. That passage to Me

The Gift of the Eternal Father

brings you into spiritual childhood and is a pure gift of Love.

Daughter, pray much for the human family to be converted by that yoke that is light, the cross that He bore in fulfillment of His mission. Mankind had fallen from grace but is restored by the Blood of the Lamb because of the love We have for you. Pray that the unity of the Most Holy Trinity be reflected in the family of mankind. It is by communion with Him in the power of the Spirit that you find rest and peace.

Daily humble yourself beneath the yoke of His Gospel and in meekness of heart become patient and merciful like Him. He makes His Father known and glorified on earth by generating His image in you. Then you become like Him in love. My Son is divine graciousness reflecting the unspeakable goodness of His Beloved Father. He said you must become perfect as your Father in heaven is perfect. The Holy Spirit will perfect and present you to Me through the Heart of the Redeemer. He knows best how to honor His Father and your Father. I love you, The Eternal Father.

☩

August 6, 2004   Feast of the Transfiguration
I Testify to My Beloved Son

The Eternal Father began, Daughter, come, listen and write. On Tabor's Mount, He transfigured into the Glory that is His! Peter, James and John bore witness to His glorified being so they would give testimony to the love I have for My Only Begotten Son. They heard my words: "This is My Beloved Son, listen to Him."

I confirmed the Truth and bore witness to the Word Incarnate who is my most beloved Son, one with me in the power of the Holy Spirit. To say that my favor rests upon Him means that He possess all that I have for we are two persons, one Supreme Being, together with the Holy Spirit. I am telling you to listen to Him because He is the full revelation of Divine Charity and you are made for such revelation. I do not ordain that you walk in darkness, but have given you the light of day, the revelation of the love of the Trinity, and His name is Jesus. In the beginning I AM spoke His Word saying, "Let there be light" and creation came into being from the utterance of the Word of God. I broke the silence of Love's abode to generate a family and every utterance of Mine is for the sake of your good and My glory. Every Word that comes from the mouth of God is life-giving, creative charity that beautifies creation to glorify My Name.

Heed His word and understand that listening to Him is an act of surrender. When you listen to Him you are not speaking rather you are receiving the gift of His Presence and instruction into your heart poised in the posture of listening. Understand that listening to Him requires humility because only the humble have ears for spiritual communication and hearing the Word of God requires obedient faith to believe and do whatever He tells. This is why the art of listening is best understood by the little children of Mary Most Holy.

Did she not echo my own words at Tabor when at the Wedding Feast at Cana? She said, "Do whatever he tells you." This expression is repeated by her and stands as one of the few utterances of the Mother of Christ captured in the scriptures because of its profound meaning. Listening to My Son is a necessity for the soul making its way back to Me. The children of the Immaculate Heart of Mary are taught well by her holy example. Never has another human being listened more fully to Jesus Christ.

The fiat of the Mother of God is her perpetual response to the Most Holy Trinity. She is the most elevated and chosen human vessel who teaches, by example and by prophetic utterance, that revelation is a grace from God given to those who listen to Him. The holiest of Mothers instructs her children to listen to Him, to allow Him to write His gospel upon your hearts. The Holy Spirit, her most beloved Spouse, makes fruitful this instruction by the sanctifying action of His Charity transfiguring you into the image of the Son.

The transfiguration at Tabor took place in a moment in time

preceding the Perfect Sacrifice of Good Friday as a sign to strengthen His Apostles to have hope in Him. The transfiguration at Calvary is a perpetual sacrifice and His greatest glory. Is there any servant who is greater than the Master? Why would you think your personal transfiguration could be realized without following the same manner of sacrificial love as the one perfect Master? Peter, James and John were given grace at Mount Tabor so they would not succumb to the scandal of the crucifixion. Through they were paralyzed with fear until the revelation of His resurrection, the memory of His transfiguration resonated in their hearts.

On your earthly pilgrimage you also are given moments of grace, revelations of the glory of My Son, so you can endure all tribulation with the hope of the glory that is to come, the glory that is My everlasting covenant. By the power of Divine Grace, you are being transfigured moment to moment when you listen to My Son. To the degree that you open your heart to hear His Voice, you receive the ardor that consumes His soul and move into His immensity for love.

I testified to Him so that you will know He is my only begotten Son. Now creation is called to repeat my testimony proclaiming to the four corners of the earth, "Jesus is the Beloved Son of the Father!" These are costly words in a world growing daily more hostile to the Gospel and to Christians! When you listen to Him, you will suffer the insults of the world coming against Him and be persecuted for your faith in Him. He is still a scandal to the nonbeliever and the cross is still scorned by the spirit of the world. As His disciple you follow His footsteps and the path is narrow, steep and difficult. Listen to Him and you will see the glory of the Most High. Listen to Him and in the midst of the fiery ordeal that surrounds you, you will have His peace and the fortitude of a warrior. I bless you, The Eternal Father.

✟

September 8, 2004 — The Feast of The Nativity of Mary
Mary: Spotless Mirror of the Most Holy Trinity

The Eternal Father began: Daughter, come, listen and write. This day when the Universal Church celebrates the nativity of Miriam, The Virgin Mary, there is cause for utmost joy because at her birth, the winds of salvation began to blow. In her fiat to the Divine Will began your salvation and moment of triumph. She is the prime example of a perpetual fiat born of humble, obedient charity. The heavenly court resounds with hymns of gratitude for the Queen Mother of heaven and earth who freely chose to live each moment within the realm of the Divine Will. I am well pleased in her singular sanctity and dignity to be the spotless mirror of the Most Holy Trinity.

Who is this little creature, so beloved of the Most High? She is the Immaculate Conception born without stain of original sin, conceived in My Mind's Eye to be of elevated estate. She is the New Eve who obeys to become that fruitful garden and mother of the tree of life. She is the Perpetual Virgin who is pregnant by the power of the Holy Spirit, her spiritual spouse, becoming the living and most fitting tabernacle of the Word Made Flesh. She is chosen to bear the promised Messiah foretold by the prophets of old and Mother of the new and eternal Covenant of His Blood.

She is the mother of the Eucharist since on that Holy Thursday, her union with Jesus caused her to know first the meaning of His words, "This is My Body; this is My Blood". She is the Co-redemptrix at the foot of the Cross as a sword pierces her heart in union with her Son's Heart as her intercession for His offspring. The fulfillment of Simeon's prophecy is realized there. She is your mother in the order of Divine Grace given to you at Calvary by the utterance of her Son as a sign of His everlasting mercy. She is the Masterpiece of the Most High that best exemplifies the Beauty of Divine Charity, assumed into heaven to reign as Queen and Mother, a flower that continues to bloom and fragrance the environment above and below. She is the fountain of Trinitarian mercy for you. The infinite wellspring of Trinitarian Charity flows through this Immaculate Vessel to water the earth with life giving seeds of grace. Her perpetual maternal fruitfulness increases the human family's capacity to receive the love of the Trinity.

Today all three persons of the Trinity repeat Christ's words uttered from the depths of His Heart about to be pierced, "Behold your Mother"! She is sent to earth as The Queen of Prophets speaking on behalf of the Trinity to build up the Mystical Body. In every age she is with you to strengthen and guide the pilgrim Church. Today she is present to the Church Militant to lead the battle against darkness because The Evil One has deceived and blinded your generation. At the directive of the Most High she leads an army of humble children to rise up, to stand for Christ and the Gospel. Children of hers are the saints of your time.

I send her to you as gift of My Paternal Heart for you each are in need of her maternal solicitude. I send her to lead an army to claim the victory already procured by Christ Crucified and Resurrected to rescue the many people on the path to eternal defeat. I send her to form you into saints by your daily surrender as she becomes your prayer partner helping you to yield to the inspirations of the Holy Spirit. There will be more saints from this age than any other age because the Enemy of mankind is freely roaming the earth unchained, making his last stand; releasing legions from the netherworld to pursue the offspring of Mary Immaculate. You are formed by her to be soldiers in a great spiritual war against powers and principalities but you remain under the protection of Mary Immaculate and are led by the power of the Holy Spirit.

Today, you honor the Woman of the Book of Revelation, she who is more radiant than the sun and crowned with twelve stars. She is destined to crush the head of the Ancient Serpent to put an end to his terror, gathering souls who would otherwise perish for lack of faith. Through her maternal mediation will come the dawn of a new day, an age of sanctification in which you will be led by the Holy Spirit, aware of Divine Presence, consecrated in Truth, to live the Divine Will on earth. The present darkness will give way to the light of truth and you shall see the divine plan in the radiance of the Holy Spirit.

Behold your Mother and walk with her into the Light. Through her maternal mediation, darkness will be dispelled and you will be restored. Blessed are the children of the Immaculate Conception because she is your safe refuge and guiding star leading you out of the darkness of night and into the brightness of the noon day. Let your faith in Me be your sure compass.

I bless you. The Eternal Father.

I am the Immaculate Conception

✞

September 15, 2004 Feast of Our Lady of Sorrows
Mary's Maternal Cry Pierced the Heavens

The Eternal Father began, Daughter, come, listen and write. Jesus' father and mother (St. Joseph and Mary) were amazed at what was said about Him; and Simeon blessed them and said to Mary, His mother, "Behold this child is destined for the fall and rise of many in Israel, and to be a sign that will be contradicted and you yourself a sword will pierce so that the thoughts of many hearts may be revealed." (The Gospel of the day: Luke 2:33-35)

The prophecy of Simeon thus formed the sharp sword that pierced the Immaculate Heart of Mary. Through the generations, her heart is pierced again in solidarity with the Mystical Body, so the thoughts of many hearts may be revealed. Through the graces of the Cross, the Spirit of Truth revealed the thoughts of many hearts so reconciliation is realized. The seven swords of sorrow that pierced the Immaculate Conception reveal the fullness of her mystical suffering as she, above all others, united fully to the passion of her Son! The torments of My Beloved Son were experienced in the depths of the Immaculate Heart because these Two Hearts are as one in the Spirit.

The foreshadowing of the Messiah is in the old law, in the covenant revealed to the prophets. Israel anticipated a Messiah king who would reign with power and raise up Israel forever. Jesus was sent; the Messiah was born of the Virgin Mary; born to suffer, die and rise again. This Suffering Servant bore in His Body the sin of every generation! Who can fathom such agonies of body, mind and spirit?! Who can fathom the purity of such innocence to be so violated? Only Mary! That chosen vessel! She can fathom His sufferings because she participated in all His agonies spiritually. Do you understand that her heart was pierced through and torn asunder with unspeakable violence, too?

As mother, in the deep of the night, when the sins of all generations whipped up a frenzy to conspire and torture her Holy Offspring, her maternal cries pierced the heavens! What I heard from her anguished heart! Such agony! This quickened My Paternal mercy! The Choirs of Angels harkened and received her passionate cries. They sang her lamentations filling the heavens with compassionate canticles of charity. The lullabies that she once sang to her Infant Son were etched into His memory and colored His Passion with the balm of maternal affection. She moved not only His Heart, but Mine. She touched heaven and earth as no other creature could do. The angels collected the tears in the midst of her suffering to bring unto Me. They are preserved in the Crown of the Queen Mother as evidence of her offering to all Three Persons of the Trinity.

Though she suffered to the marrow of her bones, though she would have died with Jesus if she could, her agony revealed the depth of her maternal charity as she presented her pierced and broken heart to Me, saying only one word: Fiat! And this word was uttered in totality of body, mind, heart and spirit. As her heart broke into pieces like the pieces of flesh torn from the Body of her Son, her human will was fixed, as always and forever, fixed on the Divine Will. The Holy Spirit led her unceasing prayer and her prayer is summed up in one word: Fiat!

The Mother of Sorrows began her mission of Co-Redemption with the words, "Let it be done unto me according to Your Word" for this is when the winds of your salvation began to blow. She lived the essence of her fiat at each moment of her pilgrimage on earth. It can be understood that when she stood at the foot of the Cross, as her Son's heart was pierced, as blood and water flowed out, falling from the Cross onto the earth, her fiat climaxed to fertilize the earth upon which flowed her Son's Precious Blood. This is the complementary grace of maternal charity that waters the earth to make it fertile. Her nature is all human but it is a nature that is immaculately human and you are unable to comprehend the splendor of this mystery but I tell you that no one else compares to her!

Jesus was obedient even unto death on a Cross. United to her Son she mirrored His obedience. Daughter, understand that Jesus saw in His mother's fiat the reflection of His own and was strengthened in His most agonizing moments when He looked into that

Citadel of Courage; His most holy mother, so meek and humble yet zealous! There was a mutual inflammation of their charity, mirroring one another's zeal for the mission. Both were filled with the desire that My Name be glorified because of the love they have for Me.

Jesus is the one Redeemer. Mary is the first co-redeemer and mother of the children of God who forms you into other co-redeemers so the family of man is brought into union, by baptism, into that saving act that redeems humanity. The New Covenant of reconciliation is established when He was lifted up to bridge heaven and earth. His suffering gives purpose to all human suffering: it is Salvific! It is she who helped raise that Bridge in His humanity. It is His divinity that raised her humanity to be clothed with graces that bring her into participation with His divinity.

As she removed His Body from the Cross, anointed and buried Him in the tomb, the swords of suffering had pierced her thoroughly. She embraced fully the mystery of Divine Love and sighed in relief that He suffered no more. She is the first to believe that He lives and she leads mankind in faith. She understood that He has ransomed His people and fulfilled His mission as Messiah. She understood His Kingdom was not of this world. She had already buried her heart so thoroughly in His that she rested there, in that gaping wound! She rested there because she knew that pierced Heart of His was the beginning of something new. His words resounded in her spirit, "Behold, I make all things new!" Her tears had dried now; her faith was always expectant! She was trained by the Spirit to anticipate the movements of Her Beloved Son.

Assumed into heaven now, she unites her heart to the sorrows of her children on earth. The sin of the human family is always a sword of sorrow. She sees how many souls are bound by sin and risk eternal loss. Knowing the costly ransom paid for the debt of mankind, she longs to gather all souls unto the King's House for that eternal banquet prepared by Her Son. The words of her Son from the Cross, "Woman, behold your son" are etched into her heart. She beholds you, her sons and daughters in the same immaculate heart of love that beheld the Christ.

The mother of sorrows is the mirror of the Most Holy Trinity.

She is made to observe the pride and rebellion that is slung into the Face of the Most High. This forms another sword that plunges into the depths of her heart and remains as long as her children pay homage to idols and refuse to worship Me in Spirit and Truth. As a good mother she mourns the wayward children. But she is never forgetful of the lost sheep and always pursues them. Does a good mother gather or scatter? She gathers all under her mantle of grace and opens wide the door to her heart because a mother's heart is always hospitable.

As Mediatrix and Advocate she prays before the Mercy Seat on behalf of poor sinners. She is sorrowful for those children who blaspheme her Son, those who perpetuate the culture of death and lead the apostasy, profaning the Church. She anticipates your conversion and repentance bringing hope to hopeless situations. Even the smallest act of repentance or charity is magnified in her heart before coming unto Me. Only in heaven will you comprehend how much she has worked for you.

There is one sword that repeatedly pierces the Immaculate Heart and this is formed by the unspeakable sins against purity, sins of the flesh that escalate and dehumanize the body. This is the foremost cause of souls falling into the abyss! Daughter, the virtue of purity is being erased by your generation! I, who am the Architect of Life, fashioned the human body for My glory, for your good. Purity and innocence are to be esteemed and protected because they are a reflection of Divine Beauty, signifying the dignity of the human person. Sins of the flesh are a scourge to the human family! Your body is a temple of the Holy Spirit, the abode of your soul and is not your own to degrade or abuse. Divine Charity demands the flesh to be led by the Spirit and esteemed as a beautiful mirror creation of the image and likeness of Three In One.

Who is leading the way to stop such atrocities? She who is called the Immaculate Conception: she who bore in her womb, the Innocent Lamb! Your Holy Mother already suffered to see His innocence violated once and for all! Today she observes her ransomed children scourging one another with the treacherous whip of impurity, seducing one another to violate the dignity of the person, using one another in contempt of the Sacred. She sees too many souls forsake their eternal inheritance for the fleeting pleasures of the body. The culture of death is the resulting entrapment that is the cause of unspeakable suffering in the human family. The ripple effect of sins of impurity is far reaching into the human condition. It darkens humanity and pulls you down into the lowest posture next to animalistic behavior. One who is ensnared in sins of impurity cannot help but ensnare others. Then you resemble the snakes of the earth and this is not too harsh a word from Me.

Daughter, pray and sacrifice to alleviate the continuous sorrows of the Immaculate Heart. As the sword pierces her repeatedly, the thoughts of many hearts are being revealed. I hold the human heart in My Hand to sift you like wheat to determine the sheep from the goats. Nothing is hidden from Me. I see in the shadows of the darkness those who try to escape My view. All that you do in the dark will become fully exposed to the light and many will not recognize themselves anymore.

Unite your heart to the Lady of Sorrows to make reparation for sins of the flesh because this is the snare of the Hunter that entraps countless. Pray that the sheep gather close to the Good Shepherd. The hour is late and many are lost. Go with Mary to seek out the lost sheep and allow your heart to be pierced to bring them back to Me. Pray as I ask and I will hear and answer you.

Daughter, I love you, The Eternal Father.

September 22, 2004
Poverty of Spirit, Personal and Ecclesial
The Priesthood of the Lord

The eternal Father began, Daughter, come, listen and write.

Personal Poverty of Spirit

Daughter, now it is true that you are all weakness. You have been poured out in intercession for your family, united to Christ Crucified, to suffer, pray and live as another sacrificial offering to appease divine justice. I would render justice in your family but because of your sacrifice I render mercy, for you have drawn from the wellspring of the most merciful Spirit and sprinkled your loved ones with holy water. Your anguished cries resound in My ear for I am not deaf but hear clearly the cry of my children and attend to the humble and contrite heart that suffers.

In the eyes of the world you have material wealth and it is true that you want for nothing of the comforts of life. But alas! I see the poverty of your spirit and it is I, your eternal and good Father that empties you out to make you poor in spirit because only the poor in spirit can see and know Me. The material wealth that surrounds you serves a divine purpose to make your suffering invisible because heaven alone can know your sacrifice made behind the closed doors of your room. Your material wealth is a gift given that serves the Church but not your own heart. That is preserved by a special grace for My Son only.

I send the Spirit to lead you back into that Garden of decision: the Garden of Gethsemane made fertile by the blood sweat of The Lamb. There you keep company with Him in your own agonizing, continuous prayer that leads to a perpetual fiat to the Divine Will. Each visit to that Garden bears fruit in your soul. The Holy Spirit leads you back into the Garden of decision and My Son asks you again, "Can you drink the cup?" You have learned that the Chalice is accompanied by grace so quickly the Spirit strengthens your resolve to drink of the Cup offered. This exercise of docility to the Spirit, of obedience to the Divine Will, produces the virtue of charity in your soul. It is that gem, the crown jewel of all virtue that magnifies the Word Incarnate and radiates the Holy Spirit for the Church.

Daughter, understand that I empty you only to fill you with virtue that mirrors the Immaculate Daughter of the Most High. Now when I see you so poor in spirit and weak from suffering, I draw you closer to Me and feed you spiritual food, giving a generous portion because I have found you to be generous with Me. When I strip away that which you would like to enjoy on earth, I do so for the intent purpose of giving you something far superior and imperishable! You were chosen from the beginning but of your own volition you were found wandering independently, weighed down with self love, ingesting the spirit of the world. I found you like a lamb that left the flock, wandered off from the loving embrace of the Good Shepherd and drinking from the deadly pool of pride.

From the beginning you were made for My paternal charity and The Good Shepherd needed only to breathe upon you, one powerful sigh of Divine Love for you to recognize yourself in the Truth. In that moment you and Truth embraced and you were set free to live the Divine Will. Daughter, you have never forsaken that initial call to conversion but continue to bear the weight of responsibility as a courageous soldier for Christ. While on earth you will carry the Cross as another co-redeemer, another sacrificial lamb, so that in heaven, great will be your reward and with the elect you will partake in that eternal banquet that is the Wedding Feast of the Lamb. Proceed now to listen and write because I will reach many people through these encounters.

Ecclesial Poverty of Spirit
The Priesthood of the Lord

Jesus summoned The Twelve and gave them power and authority over all demons and to cure diseases, and he sent them to proclaim the Kingdom of God and to heal the sick. He said to them, "Take nothing for the journey; neither walking stick, nor sack, nor food, nor money and let no one take a second tunic. Whatever house you enter, stay there and leave from there. And as for those who do not welcome you, when you leave that town, shake the dust from your feet in testimony against them." Then they set out and went from village to village proclaiming the Good News and curing diseases everywhere. (The Gospel of the day: Luke 9:1-6)

The Twelve represent the priesthood of the Lord and to them is given power and authority over all demons and to cure diseases and they are sent to proclaim the Kingdom of God and to heal the sick. Behold! The priesthood of Jesus, in your age, is anemic for lack of holiness and they have failed to carry out that which they are so highly chosen to do for the Mystical Body! Look around and see the sick of body and soul who search for a cure and find none because so many who bear the sacramental stamp of the Royal Priesthood are blinded by pride and bound up in chains of worldliness. They, who are the physicians in the Church, are in need of medicine for themselves.

See, daughter, they look in the mirror and see only themselves because they have been led to the pool of self importance and drink of the poison of independence. Rare are those men who see in the mirror the reflection of Christ Crucified and recognize themselves to be like Him, embracing the fullness of victim-hood, that call to perpetuate His most charitable and pierced Heart! The remedy for the Priesthood in your age is nothing less than full identification with Christ Crucified and this means they drink the chalice to the dregs, denying themselves, and taking up daily the Cross of self denial to rest upon that Wood that is reparation for sin.

And these chosen and anointed men should leave behind all worldliness, for wealth has been the downfall of many. They should embrace poverty of spirit to resemble the God-Man who emptied Himself. They should reach out to one another to lift themselves up, one by one, onto that Cross so they become united with the Eternal High Priest on the Bridge that He formed between heaven and earth. From this vantage point, and only from this vantage point, should they offer sacrifice on behalf of the people of God. Only through their union with Christ Crucified do they become Eucharistic bread for the life of the Church. Charity is lacking in the Church because the priesthood of Jesus is being refashioned in the face of modernity to be emptied of the Sacrifice. But Christ is the same yesterday, today and forever and Truth is revealed once and for all so the priesthood of Jesus Christ is established for all ages and is summed up in the person of Jesus Himself.

When the person of Jesus lives and reigns in the person of the priest, the Kingdom of God is at hand and The Mystical Body has The Physician who takes authority over unclean spirits and cures the sick of body, mind and spirit. He said to them, "Take nothing for the journey" and this indicates spiritual childhood, dependence upon the Eternal High Priest that makes possible the virtue of humility in His priest sons. This virtue of humility is that all important extension of Divine Charity for the God-Man humbled Himself to become the servant of all. The priesthood of the Lord will be renewed when these of vessels of election humble themselves and become obedient, taking their rightful place in Christ Crucified, drinking of the cup of His holiness to live the Divine Will. The priest is the consecrated hand of Jesus. Christ's hand is immaculate, undefiled! In Him, the priesthood is made pure also for the One who is undefiled, takes away the defilement of these men through whom He manifests His Priestly Life.

Keep a prayerful vigil for the purification of all priestly hands and bathe them in tears of intercession. Pray for these chosen men in need of continuous sanctification so they rightly exercise authority given unto them in the person of Jesus. Countless souls await their priestly ministry for healing and freedom from bondage of sin and evil.

I desire that priests begin anew and reserve the necessary grace to regenerate the life of Christ in them. In turn, they will set free those people who walk in the bondage of sin and darkness of worldliness. To these chosen few, this Brotherhood so beloved of Him! and of Me! is given inestimable grace and mercy! Great and unique is their responsibility in the Body of Christ.

Daughter, when you see the Royal Priesthood compromised by the weakness of a man, invoke the Holy Spirit to stir up the fire of divine love that first pierced his heart and opened him to the divine call on his life. By this means that purifying Fire will regenerate life in him. Your suffering on earth becomes a healing salve for the priesthood because of your union with the One Eternal High Priest. The Church will be restored and led by His Eucharistic Heart and those consecrated hands of His Priesthood shall become holy by the fire and water of the Spirit. The little brides of Christ, little mirrors of Mary Most Holy, intercede to draw mercy upon His priesthood. The Heart of the Redeemer will not delay His own infinite yearning to heal His priesthood. His prayer for unity shall be fulfilled as He brings them together to strengthen one another, to know of their need for one another. He will make them a brotherhood in His Sacred Heart and show mercy because they have suffered much and are in desperate need to be re-united in Him to begin again in purity of heart, spiritually poor and thirsty for Love.

Daughter, courage, perseverance and peace are with you. I love you, The Eternal Father.

✝

September 23, 2004 Feast of St. Pio
St. Pio: As If It Were His First, Only and Last Mass

The Eternal Father began, Daughter, come, listen and write. This day the Church honors a priest who has been raised to the altar of sainthood because it is the duty of the Church to bring before her people the lives of exemplary sanctity. St. Pio is for you, an intercessor and example of a victim of Divine Love who bore the imprint of Christ Crucified. His priesthood is a signpost that points to the royal road of the Cross. By his sufferings in union with Christ he drew grace upon his spiritual children, especially his priest brothers whom he so loved.

He was fashioned into another Christ at a particular time in the history of the Church to be a sign from Above; a pillar for your times. He prepared the way, cut a path for you to follow that cuts through the darkness of the sins of your age. As the Enemy tempts the Church to take the low and easy road, I set before you an example to follow. I give you an ordinary priest infused with extraordinary charisms, to point back to the straight, narrow and steep road of sanctification. When the Priesthood of the Lord would become infiltrated with the ease of the world, I raised up a priest who would have nothing to do with worldliness or ease. When the Priesthood would be tempted to forget the sacrificial nature of perfect charity, I gave you a priest who would show you the visible wounds of My Son and intercede through suffering to aid priests' transformation. He magnified Christ Crucified to radiate divine mercy in the Church and the first recipients of this merciful outpouring are his brother priests.

St. Pio measured himself next to the standard of the Cross and strove only to climb that Wood. He saw The Cross to be his bed of transforming union. His free will inclined only toward this union. All the duties of His priesthood were seen in the light of the Cross, in the Wounds of the Beloved. He saw the souls of the faithful as targets of Divine Mercy and aimed to pour Christ's mercy into the hearts that turned to him. He was taken mystically beyond his time and place, glimpsing into the things that would happen in the future. He was an appointed prophet for your times whose life became a perpetual prayer. He saw the storms that would assail the Church; the way humanity would be twisted and torn. He desired that all would be saints of these times, martyrs of divine charity. The spirit of St. Francis enveloped him with the burning desire to be transformed into another Crucified One, to make a radical gift of himself as victim of Love.

Few people could know how agonizing the sufferings of this priest were as he preferred to be silent and hidden in suffering because of his profound humility. Though he suffered much and often bled profusely from the wounds that imprinted his hands, feet and side, he was a tireless priest, shepherd of souls. Contemplation animated his priesthood so he spent himself administering the sacraments and zealously guiding souls toward sanctity. Prayer was the constant stream of living water for his soul, the rosary always between his fingers, always prayed from his heart.

Understand that St. Pio knew how to drink deeply of the treasury of grace in the heart of the Church. He made the Eucharistic Sacrifice the source and summit of his priesthood and his soul would soar at the moment of Consecration when the Holy Spirit honors the invocation of the priest to change bread and wine into the Body and Blood of Jesus. He was often moved to tears or entranced because his love of this Most August Sacrament was deeply intertwined in the fabric of his being. He understood This Bread to be that food sustaining him in grace, a grace he preferred above all others because of its sublimity! Few priests have penetrated the mystery of the Eucharist as he did. He was led by the Holy Spirit to plumb the depths of the Eucharistic Heart of Jesus.

He loved His Master and King, and longed for communion with Him; desiring never to be separated from Him. The Holy Sacrifice of the Mass is that most intimate of moments, the most sublime occasion of union with the Beloved. St. Pio knew well how to ingest the Bread of Life and live. He approached the altar as if it were his first Mass, his only Mass and his last Mass! As priest he brought to the altar the gift of Christ's wounds; a gift from Above, to perpetuate the Sacrifice of Calvary as an offering on behalf of the people. Each prayer uttered from his lips sprang from the depths of his priestly heart that was already pierced for love of the God-Man. He had offered himself as a young man, and even as a child was united to Christ in a unique way that prefigured the graces that would flower in his years as priest. From his youth, the Virgin Mary had captured his heart for her Son.

The communion of saints is an important portion of the treasury in the Church and you do well to avail yourself of their richness as teachers, intercessors, and guiding lights along the pilgrim road. St. Pio is a particular sign of the times you are living. Contemplating his life, you will discover indications of things to come as his priesthood was conformed intimately to the Cross, and he was made to share in Christ's Passion to make present My Son's mercy. St. Pio did not choose the direction of his journey but he was led by the breath of the Spirit. He surrendered unto the Divine Will and was obedient to those in authority over him. These things he did with the utmost self-deprecation, even self-contempt. He was blinded to the luminous radiance of his own countenance and thought himself to be the least of all priests. He relied on his brother priests for spiritual direction and desired only to serve them in all humility as a poor friar.

Understand that his greatest virtue on earth was his thirst for the God-Man and charity for poor souls. His priestly heart was pierced repeatedly as he was consumed by the Fire within. Yet he was rejuvenated constantly by the same Holy Spirit. His pierced hands and feet were painful wounds of love by which he interceded to heal the wounds of souls in the greatest of need. The sacred markings on his body were to bless you, the Church, with the visible presence of another Christ, so that your own faith, hope and love would be enkindled.

He found consolation in nothing outside of the Cross because suffering was his gift to Me. He wanted only to imitate the God-Man who had captured his heart from the beginning. He knew well that Jesus came to glorify Me on earth and he set out to bring glory to My House by his self immolation. The Spirit led him through the dark night of the soul and spirit, and in the night of faith, he persevered. The Spirit drove him into the desert to wrestle with Lucifer and legions so he engaged in spiritual battles but always with the help of his Holy Mother and ministering angels. He did not fight for the sake of his soul only but on behalf of faithful souls and the forgotten souls in Purgatory. He engaged in spiritual warfare for his beloved Franciscan Order, the priesthood and Pope. He lived for Jesus and others, with selfless abandonment to Divine Providence even when it appeared that he was utterly rejected by his own and sent apart to suffer alone.

St. Pio is raised up as a sign for the world, showing an authentic priest victim to be a revelation of Divine Mercy, a fruitful tree that remains. Take solace in the example of St. Pio and honor him as a mirror of Christ. See a humble, charismatic priest who was sanctified by his suffering, persevering to run the race to win. He was a fisher of men, catching many souls for the honor and glory of My kingdom. Follow the way of the saints, standing on their shoulders to build up the Church. Their lives are diverse to show you the many facets of Divine Love and each journey is unique. Know that I choose you to become a saint also.

Daughter, your intercession for the Church and priesthood is simply an extension of maternal mediation. The Immaculate Heart has formed you for the service of your family and Church and I have chosen you for My Son. Remain close to the Good Shepherd. By your union with Him you are sanctified and fulfill your mission as intercessory victim of Love. In the eyes of some, you are judged a fool for Christ. Others see the anointing of the Spirit that accompanies your ministry in the Church. It matters not what other think, child. I, your Eternal Father, see everything and am pleased with your fiat to the Divine Will that demands the embrace of your Cross. Onward, my child! Don't look back. Courage, little one! I love you, The Eternal Father.

✟

September 27, 2004
Whoever Receives This Child in My Name
Disrespect for Life

    The Eternal Father began: Daughter, come, listen and write. An argument arose among the disciples about which of them were the greatest. Jesus realized the intention of their hearts and took a child and placed it by his side and said to them, "Whoever receives this child in my name receives me. For the one who is least among all of you is the one who is the greatest." (Today's Gospel: Luke 9:46-48)

    Human nature, fallen due to sin, seeks to exalt itself and seek after positions of power and influence to exercise authority over others. Even the beloved disciples of My Son Jesus, competed for their positions around Him because their understanding was still darkened due to original sin and the influence of the Old Law. How often Jesus would illustrate for them the importance of receiving the little ones: children, the lowly, poor, aged, forgotten, and the least of their brethren. Jesus said the least among all of you is the one who is the greatest because this is the beatitude of charity, the blessedness of humility.

    Far above your ways are My ways, and the least among you who count for nothing in the eyes of the world, are most valuable and worthy to be the greatest in My kingdom because you did not sully yourselves with haughty attitudes of superiority on earth. Nor do you wallow in the poisonous pool of pride. Humility is the garment of the lowly; and sweet innocence the adornment of a child. The one who serves these is the greatest among you and worthy of everlasting divine favor. Only a child can depend upon a Father, and I am The Father you can depend upon.

Disrespect for Life

Daughter, ponder His words, "Whoever receives this child in my name receives me." Think of your generation and the countless children who are no longer received because of selfish sensuality or blatant greed. To receive a child in my name is to be open to the Creator of Life for I am He who fashions new life in the mother's womb. How many wombs have become barren by the choice of a woman! How many women have taken for granted their fertility and toyed with nature to make themselves a little god who can create or destroy according to their human calculations! Your generation has the utmost disrespect for life and disregards the creative nature of the Almighty from whom all life begins. I watch and observe a generation of scientists, doctors, researchers, lawmakers, who make themselves little gods, tinkering with the creation of a human being. I watch and observe the selfish sensuality, the promiscuous culture that promotes contraception in various forms, the most hideous of which is that procedure that aborts the life of a child in the most violent way. That commandment, "Thou shall not kill" is now relegated to an ancient covenant that is no longer valid in modern society for the child in the womb. Now your laws are protecting the right to kill instead of the right to life and these laws effect an unholy holocaust of the littlest children and the infirm aged.

What would you have your Eternal and Good Father do in the face of such violation against the Divine Law of Charity, my daughter? The cup of Divine Justice overflows and the demands of paternal judgment cry out for vengeance! My Strong Arm is held back by the United Immaculate and Sacred Hearts and those righteous souls who join in the plea for Divine Mercy for the whole world. Soon the time will come when the dawn of Divine Justice will arise and for the many souls who lost themselves in selfish sensuality or blatant greed, it will be too late. Then whoever did not receive a child in my name will find it too late to repent because now is the time of extended Divine Mercy; now is the time for conversion and reparation for sin. Now is the time to rescue the children. Children have become the most expendable of persons.

If you have ears to hear what the Spirit is saying to the Churches, hear the cry of the unborn, un-welcomed child. And forget not the tears on the face of the aged enveloped in loneliness, neglect and risk. Hear my voice like a wind that whispers for you, the holy ones, to rise up in defense of the little ones who have no voice. For the sake of the saints among you, those few souls who drink of the wellspring of holiness and suffer yourselves unto Me for the conversion of sinners; for your sake, because of your sacrifice and union with the Redeemer, I relent for now and grant more time for mercy on earth. But a record is being made because Divine Love demands accountability. The hope of your generation is found only in the Divine Mercy. Carry souls to The Divine Mercy before the day of Justice.

Open your eyes and see there is an ocean of mercy that surrounds you and is accessible to those who honor My Name, those who have washed in the Blood of the Lamb and desire to come to life. This Ocean of Divine Mercy arises, wells up, as if to catch souls to bring you back, to bathe you in the blood ocean of the merciful Lamb.

I am the Good Father of prodigal children. I run to greet you who have squandered your inheritance on insolent living, at the cost of innocent lives. Though you have not been open to life in all its fullness, I reach to rescue you. I desire that you know the truth and correct the wrong. My arms are open to receive your repentance but the hour is late and the Just Judge is coming. The value and dignity of all life must be acknowledged and protected as I, your heavenly Father, acknowledge and protect you. I do not blot you out but My just anger arises as you blot out the children; separate and destroy the child in the womb of the mother. Motherhood is My most rejected gift of your age. If you could see the shattered lives, the rivers of tears and the flow of the blood from the innocents, you would be silent no more. Let My words move you to speak on behalf of all life.

Daughter, I bless you for writing in obedience to My will when you are weary. Go now with My paternal blessing. You can rest in the united hearts of Jesus and Mary. Pray for the coming of the kingdom of the Divine Will on earth as in heaven.

Child, I love you, The Eternal Father.

September 29, 2004
Feast of the Archangels: Michael, Gabriel and Raphael
The Archangels

The Eternal Father began, Daughter, come, listen and write. John, the beloved wrote, "War broke out in heaven; Michael and his angels battled against the dragon. The dragon and its angels fought back, but they did not prevail and there was no longer any place for them in heaven. The huge dragon, the ancient serpent, that is called the Devil and Satan, who deceived the whole world, was thrown down to the earth, and its angels were thrown down with it." (Today's first reading (abbreviated) from the Book of Revelation 12:7-9)

In the realm of the spiritual world, there are incomprehensible mysteries, glorious and terrible to human understanding except through the gift of faith; the light that comes from Me to pierce the soul with revelation of My Existence. With what perfect order I have established the heavens and earth and nothing is left to chance. All that I have created is for the glory and enjoyment of The Uncreated Godhead. Divine Charity ordains creature for Creator, united by grace, in a communion of unspeakable mutual enjoyment.

The nine angelic choirs, those magnificent intelligent spiritual beings, adorn the heavens with beauty and song, singing glorious canticles of praise, chanting, "Holy, Holy, Holy!" in unceasing adoration of The Most High. These created pure angelic spirits are the messengers who exist to do the bidding of Three in One. They carry out My holy orders to sustain creation, protecting everything above and below, carrying out the Divine Will in the realm of the spirit world.

There was a magnificent being of light and power; one close to the Throne of the King and his name was Lucifer. When his intelligence perceived the dignity I would bestow upon the human person by the grace of the Incarnation; perceiving The Word who is with Me from the beginning to assume human nature to save man and raise him to the stature of union with divinity, Lucifer rebelled. War broke out in heaven and the huge dragon, the ancient serpent, who is called the Devil and Satan, who deceived the whole world, was thrown down to earth along with his legions by that greatest angelic being named Michael meaning, "Who is like unto God".

Michael is the foremost angelic warrior defending My Throne on heaven and earth and his light is impervious to the Enemy who continues to wage war on the children of the Most High. St. Michael is never defeated but always victorious for the children of the Woman of the Book of Revelation, the Queen Mother of heaven and earth, whose heel is poised to crush the ancient serpent to chain him forever in the abyss of darkness.

You are given the names of three Archangels: Michael, Gabriel and Rafael and scripture reveals the mission pertaining to each heavenly Messenger so you understand with what solicitude I, your Eternal and Good Father, provide these helpers and countless more, to bless and protect your coming and going, to aid you in discerning and carrying out the Divine Will. Every grace is from Above to aid you in your pilgrimage back to the Fatherland. In that Garden of Eden all good things were freely given and within your first parents' reach, until they freely chose to disobey seeking after My supreme knowledge. Banished from that First Garden, I had mercy upon you, My children, and sent My Beloved Son to reconcile the human family, opening the gates to paradise again.

In every phase of human history, through the course of creation, salvation and sanctification, there is the intervention and support of angelic beings to aid mankind. St. Michael continues to war against that ancient serpent defending the offspring of the Woman Clothed with the Sun. This battle escalates in your present age because that serpent roams with legions as hell is unleashed on earth to test people in these times of decision and transition. St. Gabriel continues to announce the Divine Will in the souls of the faithful carrying revelation and grace from Above. St. Raphael continues to awaken and lead people in the way of blessedness and healing, leading you from glory to glory.

Countless angelic beings take their assigned positions in the universe as protectors and bearers of Light in service of the Divine and human family. The archangels exist in the perpetual light of the Beatific Vision and are vessels of paternal charity for the family of man. I have provided everything for My creatures, every necessary and good thing! Of Beauty and Goodness, Eternal Charity, I Am! I am the Perfect, Eternal and Omnipotent Father but I bend to creation; I reach for you because of the love I have for you. I am Majestic and seek to clothe you in My Majesty. I offer you the imperishable glory of eternal life and assign angelic beings to aid you in not losing your immortal souls.

Would that My people come unto Me to experience the embrace of a Good Father! Would that you humble yourselves to receive My Vastness leaving behind the wasteland of earthly pleasures to receive from My Hand, imperishable riches; eating at My table that food of eternal beatitude. I have prepared a banquet of sumptuous fare but the grace I offer is left untouched and falls to your feet to be trampled underfoot in your haste to pursue your own way of life. I repeatedly reveal Myself to you in the person of My Son who speaks only of Me and whose Face is My Countenance, all Light! We, the Eternal Three, continue to pursue you because of Our ineffable love for you. The Divine Nature is love and nothing is stronger than the sovereign power of Divine Charity. Because the family of the Most Holy Trinity is all love and love is always relational, the Divine Fountainhead must be poured out upon you, our human family. Love is compelled to be given away, to spend itself for the beloved, and you are My beloved.

I, the Eternal Father, breathe Supreme Charity upon the whole of creation and with longing I await to unite you with Me, attaching you to the divinity that is to adorn you as we embrace in a perpetual gift of self. This is the delight of Creator and creature, and why I brought you forth from nothingness. If you but knew the gift of God! I breathe the Spirit of Life upon you, intertwining My grace with your unworthiness to transfigure you into My Light. I wait upon you, present generation! See My Truth and turn back to Me! I have made you for Myself and our communion is ordained from the beginning. At the dawn of creation, I gave you authority over the earth to subdue it and make fruitful its resources. The Holy Spirit is leading you to the restored Garden of Eden, but you look left and right and back so you are not mindful of what is straight ahead.

Daughter, your fidelity to the task of writing is an offering of your love and obedience. I bless you with the sign of the Cross and embellish you with grace. I love you, The Eternal Father.

✟

October 5, 2004
Choosing the Better Part: Contemplating Jesus

The Eternal Father began, Daughter, come, listen and write. Jesus entered a village where a woman whose name was Martha welcomed him. She had a sister named Mary who sat beside the Lord at his feet listening to him speak. Martha, burdened with much serving, came to him and said, "Lord, do you not care that my sister has left me by myself to do the serving? Tell her to help me." The Lord said to her in reply, "Martha, Martha, you are anxious and worried about many things. There is need of only one thing. Mary has chosen the better part and it will not be taken from her." (Part of the Gospel of the day: Luke 10:38-42)

Jesus is the better part and in choosing Him you are never denied access to His most charitable Heart. My Son enters each village looking for the household that will welcome Him. Perceiving that He is welcomed, He enters to bless the hospitable heart that opens the door for Him. He seeks to impart His presence: the presence of Mercy. My Beloved Son is Divine Love Personified seeking after hospitable hearts to communicate His tender mercies for the human family.

To sit at His feet is to be in the Presence of the Holy One, The Word who is with Me from the beginning. His humanity makes Him approachable because He has approached humanity first and become the bridge between humanity and divinity. The supreme gift of the Incarnation is a revelation of the dignity of the creature and the mercy of the Creator. It is the intention of the Divine Will to incorporate humanity into the Divine Family of Three. This can be realized only through the gift of the human free will accepting the intention of the divine will. The divine will is intent upon communion, the fully realized reconciliation of creature with the Creator.

It is written, "There is need of one thing only". The one necessary thing is Jesus Christ, but He can possess you only through the free gift of yourself to Him. It is not enough to say "Lord, Lord!" but you must open that citadel of your free will in accordance to His law of charity, the Gospel in full, and allow Him to enter your heart to be transformed into His nature. His personality is to become your personality. This can happen only in the most intimate of communications: the mystical exchange of your two hearts. This is choosing the better part: choosing Christ!

One who is anxious and worried about many things is denied that most fruitful encounter with the tender, merciful Heart of the Redeemer. The human heart was fashioned in My Almighty Hand, created for Me, and is restless until it enters the divinely ordained relationship of love. In this age of modernity, most hearts are filled with the spirit of the world, those tangible but perishable things that quickly occupy space in the human heart and allow no room for Him. He was sent to enter into the human heart but He finds no room within and is un-welcomed by most people. Many say you know Him but you do not know Him, could not know Him, because you have not experienced Him in the depths of your heart, so full of anxiety and busyness!

He who is The Holy One cannot enter and commune in a heart divided. If you pay homage to many idols, He will not stand as one of many whom you serve! Be singular of heart as He is, so the seeds of contemplation can flourish in you.

I have given you My Only Begotten and Eternal Son as gift of a Good Father! He was sent into all the villages of the earth. But He was not clothed in the regal garments of the King that He is, but wore a simple shepherd's garment to put you at ease. He became

The Gift of the Eternal Father

the servant of all, obedient to His mission of salvation, and choosing death on a Cross for love of you.

Still you fear to sit at His feet, to seek intimacy with Him. Yet He continues to approach you clothed in the most humble species of bread and wine changed into His Body and Blood in the perpetual sacrifice of the altar. He who is the Most August Sacrament is most unworthily received by many souls mired in sin. He who is worthy of adoration and praise is ignored in the tabernacles of the world, with only the angelic choirs to praise Him. To sit at His feet requires a childlike dependency that seeks after the Almighty. To sit at His feet is an act of faith, hope and love. Draw near Him in a posture of humility and seek after His Holy Countenance. He desires to speak to you in the language unutterable love.

You know not what you are doing if you forsake the better part of listening to Him and busy yourselves with many things that will come to a quick end. Do you not realize that great is your need to adore Him for who He is? To listen to Him is a deep requirement of your heart, an intricate necessity for your well being. He speaks to you, each person, in the depths of your heart to satisfy your need for communion. His Voice competes for your attention because He seeks to be your companion and friend as well as Redeemer and Lord!

The one who chooses the better part is never without reward. As you draw near to Him, grace carries you into a spiritual reality more beautiful than any created thing. Sit at His feet and listen to participate in the mysteries of Divine Love that fill the human heart with joy! This is the truth that sets you free from the bondage of selfishness. In contemplation and adoration of My Son in the Blessed Sacrament, you open yourself up to the most healing reception of His love.

He is My voice, the utterance of a paternal heart! He is the bridge that carries you into the Kingdom of the Divine Will where Three in One are involved in the continuous dynamism of divine charity. This is the life that He speaks of, new life in the Most Holy Trinity.

Listen to Him with an attentive mind and heart so He can effect a deep change in you. When you behold the Beloved Son of

God, you change as He imparts His charitable personality to you. Then you will be found with oil in your lamps, prepared for the Bridegroom who is coming.

I bless you in the name of the Most Holy Trinity, The Eternal Father.

✟

October 6, 2004
"Pater Noster," The Our Father

The Eternal Father began, Daughter, come, listen and write.

Jesus was praying in a certain place, and when he had finished, one of His disciples said to Him, "Lord, teach us to pray just as John taught his disciples." He said to them, "When you pray, say: Father, hallowed be your name, your Kingdom come, Give us each day our daily bread and forgive us our sins for we ourselves forgive everyone in debt to us, and do not subject us to the final test." (Gospel of the day: Luke 11:1-4)

My Son Jesus prayed and taught His disciples to pray. He addressed Me as Father knowing that He and I are one inexpressible unity of Divine Love, acknowledging our relationship as Father and Son, and taught you how to approach Me. He prayed and was always heard because of His reverence. From the beginning We are One Godhead. As the Messiah, He prayed unceasingly for you, His adopted brothers and sisters, bringing you before the Mercy Seat of your Father. Every utterance that came from Him, whether in the spoken or silent cry of His heart, resounded in My ear because of our incomprehensible unity. He cares for you, beloved creation! His charitable constancy for you is an astounding reality to be acknowledged with gratitude.

He said to His disciples, "When you pray, say, 'Father, hallowed be your name'". He instructs you to approach your Father with utmost reverence acknowledging the holiness of My Name, for I Am Who Am. He teaches you to call Me, "Abba, Father" and this indicates our relationship: for you are not orphans but My sons and daughters, the offspring of the Most High. When a pure heart utters My Name, "Abba, Father," I am there; attentive, responsive, never deaf to your cry, hearing you before the words leave your lips. I am compelled to listen and respond lovingly to the uplifted heart of a child of Mine.

He said to His disciples, "When you pray, say, 'your kingdom come.'" He teaches you to invoke the coming of the kingdom that is not of the world as you know it, but of the Spirit. The kingdom of the Spirit is established on earth through the Person of My Son Jesus who is the totality of Divine Revelation. By the Holy Spirit renewing the face of the earth, human history moves from the act of creation, to the act of salvation, toward the era of sanctification, the age of the Holy Spirit.

Jesus established the Church to be your Holy Mother and her heart is a treasury, containing the deposit of faith so you are led by Divine Providence toward sanctification and the establishment of the kingdom of the Divine Will on earth as in heaven. The Holy Spirit is the Divine Architect of My kingdom come. He breathes purifying fire upon the earth to prepare you for what is coming, already being heralded by the trumpet blast of the angelic guardians. All around you are signs of the times, signs of the coming of the kingdom of the divine will.

He said to His disciples, "When you pray, say, 'Give us each day our daily bread.'" The bread he speaks of is twofold and each is manifold in its necessity: bread for your body and bread for your soul, one perishable and one imperishable reality that facilitates your existence; one far superior to the other. Not by bread alone does man live but by that imperishable Substance that is the Word of God, the Incarnate Heart of the Redeemer that becomes your food of everlasting life. This is the Bread that sustains you in grace and unless you eat of this Bread come down from heaven, you shall not live forever. You are created in the integrity of body and soul and I, your Good Father, provide for your physical and spiritual needs. The sustenance for your spiritual well being is ordained from Divine Mercy and is called Eucharist. The Eucharist is the Resurrected Heart of My Son and the source of all life in the Church. Your understanding of so great a gift is veiled on earth, but through faith you can penetrate more deeply the rich mystery of the August Sacrament that remains with you to give new and eternal life.

He said to His disciples, "When you pray, say, 'Forgive us our sins for we ourselves forgive everyone in debt to us.'" This is the virtue of mercy asked for and received. Your duty is to seek forgiveness and to give forgiveness. All men sin and are in need of forgiveness and this is why the Lamb shed His Blood. Just as you have received mercy at the spilling of the Blood of My Son, you must forgive one another at all cost to self and harbor no un-forgiveness of heart. If you are unwilling to forgive as you have been forgiven, you will succumb to a poison that is deadly, that drains life from you, and this poison is called un-forgiveness. If you persist to drink of this deadly poison, you will no longer recognize yourself as a child of God because you cannot draw mercy from Me. When you exact only strict justice against your brother or sister, I am your Just Judge and your own sins are not forgiven but written in My book for that day when you appear in My Court. No one can withstand My Justice and this is why Jesus said, pray that your sins be forgiven as you forgive others.

He said to his disciples, "When you pray, say, 'Do not subject us to the final test.'"

The final test is that trial at the hand of the Enemy of all souls. The Evil One is free to convict you of all your sins after first enticing you to fall into his trap to lead you away from Me. "Father, deliver us from Evil!" is the cry of a pure heart, the prayer of a person who knows the truth and is not blind to the reality of the Evil One. He who is called the Deceiver is a liar from the beginning and in every age he persists to lead souls into the abyss of darkness, to eternally separate you from Me. He who is called the Thief will rob you of your inheritance as a child of the Most High if you are not vigilant in fighting against his evil temptations that always violate the law of divine charity. I will defend you as My own and deliver you from the Evil One if you remain in My grace.

The Gift of the Eternal Father

You are clothed with power from Above to overcome temptation, to subdue yourself and conquer Evil One. I give every necessary grace and there is nothing to fear because I hold you in My Love. Only you can remove yourself from Me to wander off and build your house on sand that will not withstand the final test.

There is one perfect person of prayer and His Name is Jesus, Savior of the World. I receive all prayer through His Heart. When you pray as He taught you, I hear your prayer as coming from His Heart. It is He who has taught you how to pray. And He prays with you to Me. In the power of the Holy Spirit, you are perfected to pray according to the divine will.

I, your Eternal Father bless you in the name of the Most Holy Trinity.

✟

October 10, 2004
The Graces of Healing and Gratitude

The Eternal Father began, Daughter, come, listen and write. It is written, "As Jesus continued His journey to Jerusalem, and He traveled through Samaria and Galilee. As He was entering a village, ten lepers met him. They stood at a distance from him and raised their voices, saying, "Jesus, Master! Have pity on us!" And when he saw them, he said, "Go, and show yourselves to the priests." As they were going they were cleansed. And one of them, realizing he had been healed, returned, glorifying God in a loud voice; and he fell at the feet of Jesus and thanked him. He was a Samaritan. Jesus said in reply, "Ten were cleansed, were they not? Where are the other nine? Has none but this foreigner returned to give thanks to God?" Then he said to him, "Stand up and go; your faith has saved you." (Gospel of the day; Luke 17:1-19)

The Gospel presents the healing ministry of My Son, Jesus who heals because He loves; who works signs and wonders because He is sent to build up faith in the sovereignty of God. Faith that comes from hearing is augmented by a multitude of signs and wonders worked by the God-Man. Sickness of body, mind and spirit is cured at the command of the Son of God who is Mercy Incarnate for the glory of My Name, for the sake of all people. Whoever listens to Him and believes in His word, receives the fullness of mercy and becomes healed by faith in Him.

Faith in Him is not the only criterion to receive divine mercy. You have only to look at Lazarus who was raised from the dead to understand that Lazarus' faith did not save him, but the mercy of the Son of God. It is true that Lazarus' relatives and friends believed in Jesus and their pleading touched the tender heart of the Lord. Life is from the Creator and healing, a gratuitous gift of grace that strengthens faith.

By faith you come to understand the Person of My Son Jesus through the hearing of the gospels, tradition and teaching of the Church He established on earth. By the power of the Holy Spirit, such knowledge informs the human heart that He is the One, the True, the Good and the Beautiful, worthy to be loved and believed. By the light of faith, by the power of the Holy Spirit's action in the soul, the disciple of the Beloved grows from stage to stage of spiritual relationship and communion. Gratitude rises up from a soul through the experiential knowledge of My Son.

It can be understood that a person's gratitude is the fruit of humility and humility, the imprint of truth in the heart. The person who is thankful to My Son acknowledges the truth of what he has received as free gift of divine charity. Gratitude overflows the humble heart creating the oil of gladness that inebriates the soul, rendering it supple, to receive more grace. The art of loving, the spiritual communication between Jesus and you, builds up vitality in the human heart so that gratitude becomes a living stream to prevent hardness of heart. Gratitude permeates a healthy heart and prevents hardness of heart.

The prayer of gratitude most thoroughly mirrors the canticles of the angels, the songs of the angelic choirs that fill the heavens. The voices of the Church Triumphant, the community of the saints in heaven, harmonize with the angelic choirs to give praise, honor and glory to the Most Holy Trinity. This is a sublime orchestra of purest gratitude, fruit of the everlasting virtue of charity that permeates the realm of the Spirit. The perfected charity of all who live in heaven creates a symphony of gratitude, constant appreciation for the gift of Divine Charity.

The purest prayer of the human heart arises from a spirit of perpetual gratitude. This gratitude is multifaceted, able to see the goodness of everything that comes from Above, able to discern what is of Grace and able to make a return unto Me for all things issuing from Paternal Love. You know that everything good is a grace from the Thrice Holy One and worthy of your perpetual gratitude; but, this a secret of the saints who have become forgetful of self, who do not count the cost of discipleship and live in the reality of what is True.

Ten were healed, yet only one returned to give thanks to My Son. This is a revelation of the disproportionate number of people who return gratitude for the Divine Mercy. Daily, people are healed from various maladies but credit is given to other entities or human resources. Truly, the Almighty One is the reason for each authentic spiritual and physical healing. The healing ministry of My Son Jesus continues as a perpetual sign of Divine Mercy and countless are the unseen miracles and wonders in your time and place. His divine touch is always healing for body, mind and spirit, and is always effective in cultivating more charity in you. Blessed are they who see with the eyes of the Spirit, whose hearts are supple with gratitude, able to acknowledge the reality of divine grace working to heal persons, families, nations and churches. To these, more healing is given because more healing is able to be received. The attitude of a truly humble person will be permeated with gratitude.

The proud person cannot live in a spirit of gratitude because pride is a sin that poisons the human heart, error that renders a perversion of what is true. Pride erects self idolatry that is a denial of the Creator. When you express gratitude, you do so humbly, because the essence of what is humble is perfectly ordered in gratitude.

Live in gratitude and let this be a hallmark that accompanies you on each step on the journey back to the Fatherland. Whether I send you a joy or a trial let the spirit of gratitude radiate in your surrendered heart and this will act like a magnet for more grace. Know that gratitude of the heart is a most precious offering you give Me because it is selfless. When I observe a grateful heart, I see in you, the countenance of My Beloved Son and the humility of Mary, who professed her gratitude so eloquently in her hymn of praise, the Magnificat.

I, your Good Father, give the graces needed to attain the goal of your sanctification. Learn to pray in the power of the Spirit with utmost gratitude. Delight Me with canticles of thanksgiving in perpetual remembrance of the good things I have done in and for you. Realize that few souls offer a sacrifice of praise in gratitude of divine mercy. I am most pleased to receive such a sacrifice on behalf of the many who fail to recognize My charity and never return to give thanks for the gift of My Son and the gift of the Holy Spirit.

Daughter, move only in tandem with the Holy Spirit and He will lead your heartfelt prayer of gratitude. Seek to please Me and I will give you the gift of perseverance in prayer and peace the world cannot give. I bless you, dear child. I love you, The Eternal Father.

✝

November 2, 2004, The Feast of All Souls
The Divine Will

The Eternal Father began, Daughter, come, listen and write. Jesus said to the crowds: "Everything that the Father gives me will come to me, and I will not reject anyone who comes to me, because I came down from heaven not to do my own will but the will of the one who sent me. And this is the will of the one who sent me that I should not lose anything of what he gave me, but that I should raise it up on the last day. For this is the will of my Father: that everyone who sees the Son and believes in him may have eternal life, and I shall raise him upon the last day." (The Gospel of the day: John: 6:37-40)

He came down from heaven not to do His own will but the will of the One who sent Him and in this I am glorified. He who is the Word Incarnate is obedient in the unity of the Divine Will for love of His Father, for love of creatures, because the Divine Will is the most loving dynamism of Three in One. He teaches you the will of your Father; that everyone who sees the Son and believes in Him may have eternal life.

Today, the Universal Church honors "All Souls" as a perpetual feast of remembrance of the beloved souls of the faithful departed. Blessed are you who have seen the Son and believed in Him as the Church has taught you well to know and believe in Him so that you may have eternal life in Him. From the beginning you are baptized into His death so you participate fully in His resurrection to life. Remember that My Son has swallowed up death and that you shall live eternally in Him if you believe in Him and keep His word. For this He was sent, suffered and died, that you may not know death, but live in eternal communion with your Creator. I do not take pleasure in the death of a sinner but call you each to eternal life in Me. This is the will of your Father who is the living God that calls forth life, only life!

Life is a sacred gift born of the Divine Will and the creative act of divine charity that does not end, but continues into eternity. The final destination of your soul, however, is based upon your unity with the Divine Will as you are always free to reject the promise of eternal life by rejecting My Son Jesus.

I created the most perfect living thing: mankind, in the image and likeness of Myself. Life is something precious in My sight and you are created to be in the land of the living. I am not glorified in anything dead because Love is always fruitful and only life can be fruitful according to the love you bear for God and neighbor.

Life is a fragile reality of sublime nature and death is part of the nature of life and all are subject to it. Your breath of life is a gift of God, but your respirations are numbered so that you pass through death's door to enter new life, a life in the Spirit, in a paradise prepared for you. The faithful disciple who fights the good fight to the end receives the crown of everlasting glory. You would do well to remember that you are destined for the glory of eternal paradise.

The Church is your good Mother and true is Her teaching to honor those who have passed beyond the veil of earthly exile to enter into their eternal reward. The Church prays for these souls because her prayer draws grace from The Mercy Seat and souls receive help because of your act of charity. In faith, you acknowledge the spiritual needs of departed souls and intercede for them.

The choice is always before you, My beloved creation; the choice between life and death. I, your Eternal Father, beseech you to choose Life because I am the God of the living and the dead reside in an abyss far from the living. No one can cross from that abyss to the other side where the tree of life is planted and fruitful. The faithful are no longer subject to the limits of the flesh as you pass through death unharmed to live forever in Him. You, who live in Christ die in Him to rise in Him. This is the will of your Eternal Father.

Jesus bestowed His life upon you freely because of the love He has for Me and for you. He lays down His life only to take it up again. You also lay down your life only to take it up again if you live in His Love. Jesus, dead and risen is the Prince of Life and your mission as Church is to announce His life to all people. Eternal Life is the fruit of His resurrection and you are chosen to eat of this fruit.

At the time of death, one can see God face to face and this beatific vision is the essence of eternal life in the embrace of Three in One. On earth you see as through a veil yet through the eyes of faith, this veil can become very transparent.

Beloved, pray for the will of your Father to be done on earth as in heaven so the kingdom of the Divine Will springs forth. In this way, the Spirit will renew the face of earth and many who would otherwise perish for lack of faith, hope and love will come to life in Christ. I will to show mercy, My Son wills to make all things

The Gift of the Eternal Father

new, and the Holy Spirit wills to be the divine agent of the transformation. Know that I, your Eternal Father, love all that is created and sustained in My Fatherly Bosom.

Daughter, you have been diligent in doing as I ask. I bless you and remain with you in a bond of paternal affection. You have come to know Me as your Father in these encounters and I have shown that you are My child. I am well pleased in your obedience and love. I know the desires of your heart and will provide for you and your family. Persevere to raise high the Cross. Pray and draw mercy upon your family, the Church, and world by a life of sacrificial charity. I am with you.

I love you, My child, The Eternal Father.

Chapter Two

Prelude to Thirty-three Encounters

July, 1994
A Special Prayer to the Eternal Father

November, 1994
Paternal Wisdom on Unity in the Church

February, 1995
Paternal Wisdom on Loving Christ & Resisting the Evil One

May 9, 1995
Paternal Wisdom on America

February, 1996
Paternal Wisdom on Divine Justice, Divine Mercy

October, 1997
Paternal Wisdom on Surrender

June, 1998
Paternal Wisdom on the Eucharist and Priesthood

Closing Prayers

St. Peter Julian Eymard
Eucharistic & Marian Prayer

St. Ignatius Loyola
Mystical Intuitions of the Trinity during the Eucharistic Celebration

St. Catherine of Siena
The Trinity's Co-presence in the Consecrated Elements

The Prayer of Jesus to the Eternal Father, John 17: 1-26

The Father's Loving Sacrifice, Meditation on the Gift of God

July, 1994
A Special Prayer to the Eternal Father

The Lord Jesus taught me to pray, Come child, I will teach you how to pray to the Father saying: Abba, Eternal God Almighty, I beg of You, the grace to know the sufferings of the Sacrificial Lamb which You sent into the world as ransom for the sin of mankind. Permit me, Father, to enter the agony of Gethsemane, the humiliation of the Scourging, the mockery of the Crown of Thorns, the heavy weight of the Cross of man's sin. Having tasted the bitter cup of rejection let me taste of His death on the Cross, all for love of You and love of souls. Permit me this, Eternal Father that I may be one with The Lamb experiencing a portion of His agony; that I may do as He did, lay down my life for others.

Father, I offer You the dust that I am. Form me by Your heavenly breath into the altar of Your sacrifice. Allow me to burn like incense so the fragrance of my love arises to Your heavenly throne. When you breathe in this fragrance recognize it as having come from You, through me, as offering for souls. Take my life, Father, and cause me to glorify You.

You so loved the world that you sent Your begotten Son to save us, and we crucified Him. Now, knowing and loving Him as I do, I desire to walk in His holy footsteps to Calvary. Permit me to gather souls for You. In this way allow me to glorify Your Holy Name. Make my heart one with the Sacred Heart of Jesus forever. I offer you my free will. I offer to work all the days of my life for the good of souls, working from within the Immaculate Heart of Mary, my Mother, who aids me. I will lay down my life that souls come to know of Your Love, as you intended from the beginning of all ages.

O Father, one day your people will indeed glorify Your Name in unity and in love. Your Kingdom shall come! Your Will shall be done! Father, Your patience is astounding. Your mercy eternal! Your love, incomprehensible! Your justice, too, is mercy! Your majesty reigns in the midst of the chaos of our day. All the demons combined cannot tear down your Holy Temple! Your Truth will stand forever, unchanging and indestructible! You will preserve your faithful children for your covenant is everlasting! Nothing can separate us from Your love! Even the souls who utterly reject You, choosing death, are loved by You. You are Supreme Charity!

Abba, we are not orphans, though we walk like orphans because we have not yet understood your Sovereign Fatherhood. Gather creation into Your Divine Love, healing our misery and make us a holy people. Abba, hear the cry of your family. Transfigure us, Father!

Open the heavens to pour down Your reign, purifying creation, causing us to respond, once and for all, to Your eternal power, wisdom, truth and love! Breathe Your Holy Spirit upon us! Seal us with the sign of salvation on our foreheads so that when Jesus comes again, He will find faith on earth and pastor His own into your heavenly gates. Forever we shall adore You, Eternal God and Father Almighty! Amen.

✟

November, 1994
Paternal Wisdom on Unity in the Church

The Eternal Father began, Daughter, please write. The Church is divided. Not much longer will I endure to observe such division. I am made to observe the daily crucifixion of My Son as His Body is dismembered by division, members seeking to go apart from the Head. Apart from My Son, the Head of the Church, there is death. Daughter, pray that the Mystical Body may be one united Body, never separating from My Beloved Son.

The shepherds are rebelling and perpetuating the apostasy. Many are on the path to perdition because they have perpetuated a lie and led innocent souls astray. Many who call themselves shepherds are not of My House, not of the Good Shepherd but are like Judas! The day of justice will not relent for the rebels, the betrayers, the liars who divided the Body and defiled the Name of My Son, Jesus. My Paternal Omnipotence shall be revealed to unify and restore the House of God and her people who suffer. Prepare daily, My child. Make ready the way of the Lord. Daughter, love is the unifier. I AM leads you. Pray always and be at peace. I am your Father"

The Image Received

Then, I received the following image, as if The Father drew it for me. An arc descended from heaven to earth, symbolizing God's love which is bending down to us from heaven. Then He drew a straight line from heaven to earth. The straight line symbolized the Truth, unchanging, constant, never bending. Then He drew an arc from earth to heaven symbolizing the love God seeks from souls on earth.

So the image now looks like this: The circle is love, which bends to unite. But the Truth is in the middle, constant and never bending. For the sake of love and unity, love bends in the service of God and of one another. But the Truth remains the same yesterday, today and forever. When there is enough love, there will be unity. This is what I understood of this image.

I am moved to pray: Father, thank you for simplifying the most profound realities in the light of paternal charity. Abba, grant that I will forever be your child and be led by The Holy Spirit to pray as You ask. Be glorified in my weakness and allow others to know that I am before You as a poor sinner receiving divine mercy. Amen.

February, 1995
Paternal Wisdom on Loving Christ & Resisting the Evil One

While praying the Chaplet of Divine Mercy with my Priest Spiritual Director, I felt a sudden, intense suffering in my soul. It seemed as if the Eternal Father allowed me to mystically experience the rejection of His Beloved Son by the lukewarm or unbelievers.

The Eternal Father began, I, who am your Father impart a portion of the grief that stems from Paternal Charity as I am made to observe the pierced heart of My Son Jesus bleed profusely again in the Mystical Body. His Heart is opened wide but met with rejection and indifference still.

Also, I observe the tears of Mary Most Holy as her heart is rejected. She weeps not for herself but for you who forsake the inheritance Christ won for you. She hoped to gather you all unto her Beloved Son so He would be adored and you would be healed of a lack of Love.

I so loved the world, I sent my only begotten Son to redeem you. But you are denying Him repeatedly when you reject the Church, His Vicar on earth, His priests, His signs, His messengers, His Mother, His Spirit!

You look away from the Blessed Sacrament as if He were not really there. If you truly believed His Body, Blood, Soul and Divinity to be present in all the tabernacles in the world, why does He remain unattended and unadorned by you? Yet, He remains with you and does not close His Heart though it is spurned as in the beginning when He came to establish My kingdom. He has treated you with most tender mercies and is little loved in return.

The salvation of the world is in My Almighty Hand but your salvation is also in your free will. The world has forgotten its Creator God. I willed to have a holy family on earth but find unholy ways of men, women and children, led far from the sanctuary of the Church. I am grieved to observe what has become of you, creation. The world has seduced you away from My Son and His House and you have forsaken pure gold for perishable goods that return to dust. Like orphans you renounce what is good and embrace what is not good, coming from the Evil one.

In My mercy, I shall gather you up again to revive the Mystical Body of My Beloved Son through the arms of Mary Immaculate. Though the Evil One has caught you in his net I will free you by the omnipotent Breath of My Spirit. Seek your freedom in the good things of the Holy One and you shall be free indeed. Resist the Evil One and he will flee. He has no power over you except what you give him. I AM is speaking. Listen and be converted that you may know the love of Christ Jesus and live in Him. This will give Me glory. I love you, The Eternal Father.

☩

May, 1995
Paternal Wisdom on America

After receiving Holy Communion and after the conclusion of the Holy Mass, the Eternal Father began, Daughter, I have sent the Blessed Virgin Mary to earth as a sign of divine mercy. Her visitation is a grace and her intercession has aided aching mankind. But these graces must be cultivated or they do not bear fruit. She aids America as the Immaculate Conception bringing a holy warning and inviting conversion.

The soil of America is stained with the blood of the innocent children, their bodies crushed before passing through the womb. The air all around you is polluted with falsehood and darkness. The fiber of your culture is being torn apart. The forces of evil are waging warfare upon your Country. The purpose of such a spiritual battle is the removal of God, the separation of God from Country, from family, the breakdown of the Church established in His

Blood, especially diminishing the Sacrifice of the Altar and the strangulation of the Breath of the Holy Spirit.

Prophets repeat the warning and remedy. Turn back to Me, your God! Remain united as Church under Christ's Vicar, Pope John Paul II. As one faithful family of God, unite in prayer. Fortify yourselves with the Eucharistic Heart of the Redeemer who remains with you as Bread of Life. Repent, and divine mercy shall restore what has been lost. Gather under the mantle of the Immaculate Conception as she is a protection for life. Satan despises her because she protects life and exposes his lies. Her virtues of humility and obedience to the Divine Will drive him away for he cannot bear to remain in the presence of such unfathomable purity and holiness. She is the essence of these.

Daughter, America will be tried and put to the test soon. Difficult times are in store for this country. The greatness of America lies in My Fatherly blessing upon it. I will bless this Country again when it turns back to receive My blessing. Until such a time, there will be much to suffer. Pray much that the time of your suffering is short, that your Country will be reconciled to Me. Stand with My Son, with your Holy Mother and beget life not death. Intercede toward the day when I, your Eternal Father, may raise My Almighty hand in blessing. Then I can say, "This is holy ground again; these are repentant people. Let there be new life in America for she has seen the light of truth and embraced the Divine Will. I will raise her up as a sign to all the nations."

The spirit of death is permeating your culture and you are drinking of its poison. Slowly but surely, a spirit of death, grabs you, the family, the Church and Nation. Let the life of Christ free you to become a holy people whose charity begins with the defense of life. You can overcome the present darkness through repentance and conversion. Mercy shall be yours when you are merciful toward all life. I love you, The Eternal Father.

February, 1996
Paternal Wisdom on Divine Justice, Divine Mercy

Images

During the prayer of the rosary with my Priest Spiritual Director, I received the following images and shared them with Father. I could see two magnificent angels of brilliant light as they presented displaying a power indescribable, unlike anything I've experienced on earth. These two angelic beings were holding what appeared as large basins with something in them. Next to them were two more angelic beings holding trumpets. All four of the angels were gazing at the throne of the Eternal Father, intent only upon Him. They were in a state of preparedness and were glorifying the Eternal Father with praises of His Majesty. I found myself asking the Father, "What are you showing me?" I heard, "Child, these are the angels awaiting my command—the command to pour divine justice upon earth." I replied, "Father, what about divine mercy?" He said, "Child, observe this."

Then I saw the following images. The earth was covered by a blanket of darkness but it was pulled back like a curtain that I may see the world as if from above. I somehow observed wars, large and small, on many different continents, abortions being performed and aborted body parts strewn all over the landscape of nations, hatred among different nationalities, division in families, children without supervision turning toward the darkness, mass exodus from Churches, people betraying, destroying one another over power and greed, rampant sins of impurity and lust in public and private arenas, governments oppressing their own people, exploitation of children, confusion and fear, as if a world-wide loss of equilibrium occurred as good was presented as evil and evil was presented as good. God was mocked, His Name profaned. Man made himself a god and erected idols that mirrored the human ego.

I responded, "Father, I know of your goodness and mercy. As

you reveal this, I am overwhelmed by the godlessness on earth. What can one person do in the face of such overwhelming sin and darkness? Father, you are just and merciful but your children cry out for mercy."

The Father Corrects

The Father began, Child, I do not reveal these things so that you fall into despair or fear. You should pray and hope for purification that leads toward sanctification. One person makes a great difference. Consider Abraham, Moses and the Twelve. The faith and intercession of one man touches a multitude because I multiply the good of a just man by integrating it with divine goodness. I am a merciful Father and the trumpets have not yet sounded. I extend the time of mercy and am raising apostles of divine mercy. Proclaim it and draw from the fountain of mercy through the two hearts, Jesus and Mary, before the trumpet sounds and the cup of justice is poured upon earth. Know that divine justice is merciful.

The present darkness shall pass, the light will overcome it and the era of sanctification shall begin. This is a time of transition wherein divine mercy abounds for the asking. The key is to implore mercy and few realize the necessity of asking for mercy. One just, humble and holy soul draws mercy upon creation through the Heart of the Redeemer. Through faith, sacrifice and prayer you are formed into another intercessor to draw mercy upon those in need.

I, who am your Father, watch over creation and am offended by a lack of faith, hope and love. It is for you that I grieve. I have given this extended time of divine mercy and you should make good use of this time for repentance and conversion. Many have received the richness of divine mercy and are responsible for these graces as you are accountable for what you have received from me. Trust in your Eternal Father as I am merciful but My children have become unloving, unmerciful and what shall I do? I will do that which will correct creation and this is mercy, too.

The angels await my command as they have their mission to

carry out the Divine Will. You have the opportunity to unite to My Son on the Cross to make reparation for the sins of the human family that persist. Even the choirs of angels cannot do this. Fulfill your mission to bring souls to me by the power of divine love. Be at peace in Jesus, but do not waste time. (There was a pause and I was led to pray.)

Response and Prayer

Father, help me to trust in divine mercy and believe that one soul can make a difference in the world today. I abandon myself to Divine Providence. That you would make some good of my offering is sure proof of your mercy. You gave me the gift of faith and it is my firm foundation. I ask that you keep me in your Light that I may never cease to believe in your divine goodness. May I walk in Truth all the days of my life! For the glory of Your Holy Name, take my prayers, works, joys, sufferings, and make good use of them. Do they not originate from your own Spirit of Love?

Increase faith, hope and love on earth by virtue of the intercessory prayers and sufferings of your faithful ones. Father, all loving Creator, I cry out for those who refuse to believe, hope or love. If souls will come to know you through purification which is divine justice and mercy, then let the trumpets sound. Gather your people unto You, O God. Only in the power of the Holy Spirit will we be converted, sanctified. Let it be done according to your Word. Amen.

The Father continued, "My child, you are my beloved daughter and I will multiply your offering for many souls. Trust in my love, mercy and justice. I AM.

Prelude to Thirty-three Encounters

October, 1997
Paternal Wisdom on Surrender

At the cenacle with my Priest Spiritual Director, the Eternal Father began, My children, you are looking at the cost of discipleship without considering the reward. Great is your eternal reward if you but choose Christ Crucified and surrender. All my works are wondrous and good. If you focus on My Son, you will not count the cost of discipleship for you are created for Love and love does not count the cost. I love you with an everlasting love beyond your imagination. Whatever the cost of being a disciple of Jesus, it is a small price to pay for an eternity of glory. Your true home is with me in the Fatherland. Your earthly pilgrimage is an opportunity for you to love and be transformed into the image of My Son Jesus. The Word Incarnate is the way that leads to your eternal homeland. He is the revelation of My love for you and invites you to surrender all unto the embrace of your Abba. Walk in His footsteps and realize that no one has suffered like Him.

Do not fear to imitate Jesus on the road to Calvary knowing that I have promised the grace to carry you each step of the way. When Jesus fell along the Via Dolorosa, He got up and continued to Calvary's summit, fulfilling His mission of redemption. Surrender your lives to the One who loves you infinitely more than you can know, your Teacher and Lord, Jesus. Continue to sit at His feet so that daily you take up your cross and follow Him through Calvary to the Resurrection. Have hope! I desire for you to have joy as I, your Eternal Father, have joy in observing you. You struggle but persevere on your journey trying to please your heavenly Father. I bless you in the name of the Most Holy Trinity. I am your Eternal Father.

June, 1998
Feast of Corpus Christi
Paternal Wisdom on the Eucharist and Priesthood

The Image Received

At the beginning of the consecration of the Holy Sacrifice of the Mass, quite suddenly, I received an image of the Apostles on either side of the parish priest. The Apostles appeared to be concelebrating with the priest. Then Jesus transfigured the priest into Himself and I observed this transfiguration occur repeatedly.

The Father Explains

Suddenly, the very majestic voice of the Eternal Father began in a tone filled with authority saying: This is My Beloved Son, receive Him worthily! This is My Beloved Son, receive Him humbly! This is my beloved Son, receive Him and come to life! This is My gift to you: the gift of Paternal Love enduring forever in the gift of the Son. I am in Him and He is in Me, together with the Spirit, we are One God.

If you have repentance of sin and choose divine charity, you live in Him and He brings you to Me. I, your Eternal Father, regenerate you with the continuous gift of My Son in Blessed Sacrament. You are not a fatherless generation. I am over you providing every good and necessary thing. Hear what the Holy Spirit is saying through the Church, her invitation to gather at the Eucharistic Altar. My beloved offspring, adopted children, are wandering far from Me onto the path of destruction, forsaking the Eucharistic Heart of the Redeemer for the transient things of the world.

I remind you of the Apostles present on the first Holy Thursday, at the institution of the sacrament of love, The Eucharist. They live! They intercede on behalf of their brother priests who struggle in the midst of the evil onslaught against the Priesthood and Church.

Prelude to Thirty-three Encounters

Look to the Apostles, Patriarchs, Prophets and Fathers of the Church. Implore their help. You are in great need of their intercession. The Communion of Saints is your living resource, agents of Love, awaiting your plea for help. Let your faith be augmented by their intercession. Pray more and seek their aid in your struggles.

Blessed are you who worthily partake in the banquet of Eucharistic Love. I am bending from heaven to bring you back to My Son in the Blessed Sacrament because He is the Bread of Life and I am calling you to Life. All that you require is found in the inestimable gift of the Eucharist. The Un-bloody Sacrifice of the Altar is the perpetuation of eternal Divine Charity.

The Risen Lord remains on earth in the Sacred Host and by Holy Communion you are healed and sanctified. Let nothing keep you from the Gift of God. Ask Mary Most Holy to help you climb the summit of Eucharistic Adoration. The Eucharistic Heart of My Son is the door to Me.

I love and bless you in the name of the Most Holy Trinity. The Eternal Father.

Closing Prayers

✝

St. Peter Julian Eymard
Eucharistic & Marian Prayer

Immaculate Virgin, mother of Jesus and our mother, we invoke you under the title of Our Lady of the Blessed Sacrament because you are the mother of the Savior present in the Eucharist. From you He received the flesh and blood with which He feeds us in Holy Communion. We also invoke you under that title because the grace of the Eucharist comes to us through you since you are the channel through which God's graces reach us....

Teach us to pray the Mass as you did, to receive Holy Communion as you did, and to adore our Lord in the Blessed Sacrament with some of your love and devotion. You are the perfect lover of Our Lord in the Eucharist. Grant us the graces to know Him better, to love Him more, and to center our lives on the Eucharist.

Virgin Mary, Our Lady of the Most Holy Sacrament...pray for us and grant to all the faithful true devotion to the Holy Eucharist, that they may become worthy to receive it daily.

(St. Peter Julian Eymard: In The Light Of The Monstrance: edited by Charles Dekeyser, S.S.S., (Cleveland), 1947)

St. Ignatius Loyola
Mystical Intuitions of the Trinity During
the Eucharistic Celebration

During the Mass the tears were more copious than the previous day and lasted continuously…I knew or felt or saw, God knows, that, on speaking to the Father and seeing that He was one Person of the Blessed Trinity, I felt moved to love all the Trinity, especially as the other Persons were all in the Trinity by their very essence: the same feeling when I prayed to the Son and to the Holy Spirit; when I felt consolation I was delighted with any one of them, and I rejoiced in acknowledging it as coming from all Three.
(St. Ignatius Loyola: Personal Writings.
(Penguin Classics) pp. 82-84)

St. Catherine of Siena
The Trinity's Co-presence in the Consecrated Elements

O Trinity, eternal Trinity! Fire, abyss of love…Was it necessary that You should give even the Holy Trinity as food for souls? …You gave us not only Your Word through the Redemption and in the Eucharist, but you also gave Yourself in your fullness for your creature.
(St. Catherine of Siena: Quoted in St. Caterina Da Siena, by G. Cavallini: Le Orazioni, Orazione 20)

John 17: 1-26
The Prayer of Jesus to the Eternal Father

When Jesus had said this, He raised his eyes to heaven and said, "Father, the hour has come. Give glory to Your Son, so that Your Son may glorify You just as You gave Him authority over all people, so that He may give eternal life to all You gave to Him. Now this is eternal life, that they should know You, the only true God, and the One whom You sent, Jesus Christ. I glorified You on earth by accomplishing the work that You gave Me to do. Now glorify me, Father, with You, with the glory that I had with You before the world began.

I revealed Your name to those whom You gave Me out of the world. They belonged to You, and You gave them to me, and they have kept Your word. Now they know that everything You gave me is from You because the words You gave to me I have given to them, and they accepted them and truly understand that I came from You, and they have believed that You sent me. I pray for them, I do not pray for the world but for the ones You have given me, because they are Yours, and everything of mine is Yours and everything of Yours is mine, and I have been glorified in them. And now I will no longer be in the world, but they are in the world, while I am coming to You. Holy Father, keep them in Your name that You have given me, so that they may be one just as we are.

When I was with them I protected them in Your name that You gave me, and I guarded them, and none of them was lost except the son of destruction, in order that the scripture might be fulfilled. But now I am coming to You. I speak this in the world so that they may share My joy completely. I gave them Your word, and the world hated them, because they do no belong to the world any more than I belong to the world. I do not ask that You take them out of the world but that You keep them from the Evil One. They do not belong to the world any more than I belong to the world. Consecrate them in the truth. Your word is truth. As you sent me into the world, so I sent them into the world. And I consecrate myself for them, so that they also may be consecrated in truth.

I pray not only for them, but also for those who will believe in me through their word, so that they may all be one, as You, Father, are in me and I in You, that they also may be in Us, that the world may believe that You sent me. And I have given them the glory You gave me, so that they may be one, as we are one. I in them and You in me, that they may be brought to perfection as one; that the world may know that You sent me, and that You loved them even as You loved me.

Father, they are Your gift to me. I wish that where I am they also may be with me, that they may see my glory that You gave me, because You loved me before the foundation of the world. Righteous Father, the world also does not know You, but I know You, and they know that You sent me. I made known to them Your name and I will make it known, that the love with which You loved me may be in them and I in them.

(John 17:1-26)

Then the Eternal Father began, "This is the ideal of the Divine Will and it shall be like this for those who love as I ask. For it is written, *'This is the will of God, your sanctification.'*"

(1 Thess. 4:3)

The Father's Loving Sacrifice
Meditation on the Gift of God

Father of the Word Incarnate,
It is written: God is Love.
In your mercy, You sent Your only begotten Son.
He became the testimony of Your Covenant.
Man sinned and paradise was lost.
You willed to save man, to open heaven's gate.
You willed it and the Word became flesh.

The Gift of the Eternal Father

He dwelt among us, the Light in the darkness.
He came to His own but His own did not receive Him.
He spoke only of You and proclaimed Your Kingdom.
He bore witness to Your perfect Goodness.
He mirrored your Beauty, reflecting Your Face.
He put aside His majesty and became lowly.
He fled from riches and became poor.
He shunned His power and took on weakness.

Father of the Sacrifice,
The spotless Lamb bore our iniquities.
Clothed in garments of rejections and mockery,
He was misunderstood, betrayed and crucified.
His Blood poured out and water gushed from His side.
He gave birth to the Church through His pierced Heart.

Eternal Father, He glorified You in obedience.
And You glorified Him extending Your Kingship.
Your Covenant of Eternal Love is written.
Your Seat of Mercy is the Word Incarnate.
Your Only Begotten Son, Jesus, the Christ,
From the Cross said: "It is finished".
Redemption is accomplished, salvation won.

Heavenly Father, still, You await our fiat.
The cloak of His Precious Blood: the robe of Royalty,
Enfolds us, but only as we surrender and will it.
We must open the door of our heart.
This is the door of our human free will.

Father, Wise and Omnipotent Love!
Shower my heart with mercy and grace.
Melt my stubbornness, rebellion, and selfishness.
Pierce my darkness and annihilate my sin.
Let the Sword of the Spirit, Your Word,
Break my resistance and cowardice.
Let the flames of Eternal Love envelop my heart.

Closing Prayers

Turn stone into Living Water.
Consecrate my heart in the Truth.
Save me from my self and the world.
Draw me into Your Light.
Change me into His Image.
Write His signature all over me.
Cause me to love like Him.
Breathe His Passion into my life.
Affix my free will to the Cross that saves.
Satisfy my thirst for Love.
Then pour me out for others.

Father, Sovereign and Ineffable Love,
Look at me, so lowly a creature,
See the dust that I am and have pity!
Ransomed by the Blood of the Lamb,
Pick me up into Your Almighty Arms,
Embrace me as Your offspring, a child
Let me glorify Your Holy Name!
Abba, be glorified in your little victim of Love.

Father, eternal, creative and dynamic Love!
Speak anew, the life and power of the Cross,
Cleanse the earth by His Blood testimony.
Perpetuate His Eucharistic Heart.
Until the end of all ages, let there be Light!
Let the Victorious Lamb reign on earth as in heaven.
May His other heart, the Immaculate Conception,
Triumph with Him to gather us as one family.
Let Your Name, be hallowed on earth,
Beloved Abba, Father of us all!
On earth & in me, Your Will be done!
Amen.

About the Author

- Cradle Catholic.
- Married 30 years, mother of two sons.
- Medical Assistant, Business co-owner with her husband.
- Nominee for Catholic Woman of the Year in her diocese.
- Past President, Guild of the Lestonnac Free Medical Clinic.
- Coordinator, Magnificat, A Ministry to Catholic Women, Orange Chapter, since 1993.
- Leader of Intercessors of the Lamb Prayer Cenacle since 1994.
- Lady of the Order of the Holy Sepulchre of Jerusalem since 2002.
- Conference speaker on conversion, family issues, prayer and spirituality.
- Frequent guest of St. Joseph's Catholic Radio.
- Author, *I Will Restore You in Faith, Hope and Love*, 5 volumes, 1997-2003.
- Author, *Praying the Passion of Christ*, 2004.
- Spiritual Director since 1992: Fr. Raymond Skonezny, STL, SSL.